**KU-535-588**

Unit 3 Looping and Conditions

Prepared by the Course Team

Contents

Study guide

In the *first* unit of this block we introduced the one-dimensional array and showed how it was represented in Pascal by discussing various aspects of its use. In *Unit 2* we addressed the problems of searching arrays and introduced sorting and the idea of the efficiency of algorithms. In both of these units we made extensive use of **for** loops and **while** loops.

We use the computer to model situations and problems, to carry out processing and to assist in or to implement the solutions to problems. However, the processing speed of a computer is of limited use unless we are able to model the complexity of the tasks and problems with which we are faced. In order to be able to model any situation of interest we need to have the programming constructs which will enable us to achieve repetition and selection. You have already experienced the need for repetition and have achieved this using **for** and **while** loops. You have also used the **if** statement to carry out a selection from two options.

In *this* unit we shall discuss repetition in some detail and introduce an alternative form of the **for** loop, in which the initial value of the control variable is greater than the final value. We shall also introduce a third looping construct, the **repeat** statement, in which the condition is tested at the *end* of the loop rather than at the *beginning* as in the **while** statement. In Section 5 we shall demonstrate how the selection facility can be extended to enable a choice to be made of one option from more than two alternatives. The statement used to achieve this is the **case** statement.

At the heart of statements which achieve selection and repetition is a *condition* and we shall discuss such expressions in detail in Section 4.

After completing this unit you should be able to:

1 Understand the meaning of the terms *conditioned loop, preconditioned loop, postconditioned loop* and *counter-controlled loop.*
2 Correctly use a **repeat** statement in a Pascal program.
3 Correctly use a **for downto** statement in a Pascal program.
4 Correctly form a compound condition using the *Boolean* operations **and, or** and **not.**
5 Understand the use of the **case** statement and correctly use a **case** statement in a Pascal program.

Section 1 begins with a problem: preparing for a game of cards. The discussion and eventual solution of this problem will set the scene for the consideration of *conditioned* loops in Pascal, which is an important theme of the unit. The solution of the problem illuminates difficulties which often occur in certain kinds of situations and which are overcome by the **case** statement introduced in Section 5.

Section 2 is the longest section of the unit and we recommend that you devote two evenings to it as you will probably require some revision of topics in *Units 1* and *2* of this block.

In Section 3 we consider *conditioned loops* introducing the **repeat** statement and comparing its use with that of the **while** statement. Section 3.2 is a tape section; the cassette tape which accompanies this unit contains a commentary which directs your study of the associated material contained in the unit. Section 3 also includes a

The Open University
Mathematics:
A Second Level Course

M205
Fundamentals of Computing

Block II

Control Structures and Arrays

Unit 3 Looping and Conditions
Unit 4 More on Types

Prepared by the Course Team

The Open University Press

Course Team

Alan Best
Gordon Davies (*Chairman*)
Adam Gawronski (*ACS*)
Benedict Heal (*Academic Editor*)
Peter Leadbetter
John Newton
Jenny Preece (*Academic Editor*)
Hugh Robinson (*Academic Editor*)
Dave Sargent
David Saunders (*BBC*)
Eleanor Smith
Pete Thomas
Mike Williams (*Course Manager*)

Consultants

Jonathan Blandon
John Bramwell
Charles Easteal
Frank Lovis

External Assessor

Professor P A Samet (*University College, London*)

With assistance from:

Jonathan Davies (*Design*)
David Douglas (*Publishing Editor*)
Alison George (*Design*)
Richard Housden (*Maths*)
Diane Mole (*Design*)
M252 Tutors

The Open University Press, Walton Hall,
Milton Keynes.

First published 1988. Reprinted 1990, 1991, 1992, 1993, 1994.

Printed and bound in the United Kingdom by
Staples Printers Rochester Limited,
Neptune Close, Medway City Estate, Frindsbury,
Rochester, Kent ME2 4LT.

ISBN 0 335 14322 9

This text forms part of the correspondence element of
an Open University Second Level Course.

For general availability of supporting material referred
to in this text, please write to Open University
Educational Enterprises Limited, 12 Cofferidge Close,
Stony Stratford, Milton Keynes, MK11 1BY
Great Britain.

Further information on Open University courses may
be obtained from The Admissions Office, The Open
University, P.O. Box 48, Walton Hall, Milton Keynes
MK7 6AB.

summary of the operation of the **for** statement including the instance where the initial value is greater than the final value. Section 3 will require one evening of study.

Section 4 deals with the formation of conditions using the *Boolean* operations, **and**, **or** and **not**. The precedence, and consequently the order of evaluation of these operations, is also indicated. This section will probably require one evening of study.

Section 5 is concerned with another control structure in Pascal, the **case** statement. The usefulness of such a statement is illustrated by returning to a problem that we met in the card playing simulation in Section 2. This section will also require one evening of study.

Section 6 is a summary which contains a review of the control structures available in Pascal.

Study plan

Section	Media required	Time
1 Introduction	Text	2 evenings
2 The dynamic control of loops	Text, HCF	
3 Loops	Text + HCF, cassette player	1 evening
4 Conditions	Text + HCF	1 evening
5 Multi-path selection	Text + HCF	1 evening
Summary of unit	Text	

1 Introduction: A game of cards

Let us begin by considering the problem of simulating the playing of a game of cards. We will not concern ourselves, for the moment, with the detail of playing a particular game, but we will pave the way for such an exercise by considering the activities that often make up the preparation for a game.

Before we can begin many card games we need to choose a dealer and then deal a number of hands. In practice most people sort the cards in their hand and we may need to do this also. Of course we also need to simulate the preparation of a pack for dealing.

The two assumptions that we shall make are that we are playing with a standard pack of 52 cards, without jokers. There are four players, each of whom will be dealt 7 cards.

The first problem we face is, 'how do we represent the cards in a pack?' The method we shall adopt here is to represent the cards in the pack by the integers 1 to 52, where integers 1 to 13 represent cards of one suit, 14 to 26 another suit and so on. We shall adopt the convention that the suits will be represented in alphabetical order: clubs, diamonds, hearts and finally spades. In each suit the cards will be represented in *face value* order with ace counting low, that is in the order:

ace, 2, 3, ..., 10, jack, queen, king.

Thus, the integer 12 represents the queen of clubs, the integer 14 represents the ace of diamonds ... and so on.

SAQ 1.1

Name the cards represented by the following integers:

(i) 4   (ii) 26   (iii) 35   (iv) 50

Solution 1.1

(i)   Four of clubs
(ii) King of diamonds
(iii) Nine of hearts
(iv) Jack of spades

SAQ 1.2

Which integers would be used to represent the following cards?

(i)   Ace of spades
(ii) Seven of clubs
(iii) King of hearts
(iv) Four of diamonds

Solution 1.2

(i) 40   (ii) 7   (iii) 39   (iv) 17

With these conventions we can represent a *pack* of cards by an *array of 52 elements*. If we set up the elements of the array to be of type *Boolean*, then we immediately have a method of indicating whether or not a particular card is in the pack at any particular time. If the card is there the appropriate element of the array has the value *true*, if the card has been dealt and is not there the element has the value *false*. Thus, before we begin a deal, the pack contains all the cards and so all the elements of the array are set to *true*. When a card is dealt the appropriate element is set to *false*. For example, if the ace of hearts is dealt, element 27 of the array is set to *false*.

SAQ 1.3

The array *pack* is declared as

pack: **array**[1 . .52] **of** *Boolean*;

and before the deal begins the array is initialized by setting all of its 52 elements to *true*. If, at some subsequent time, the following elements have the value *false* name the cards which have been dealt.

(i)   *pack[16]*
(ii) *pack[38]*
(iii) *pack[42]*

Solution 1.3

(i)   The three of diamonds
(ii) The queen of hearts
(iii) The three of spades

We now have a representation for our pack of cards.

2 *Design and implementation*

2.1 Introduction

Let us now begin our task of designing the program to simulate the preparation activities. The top-level design is shown in Figure 2.1.

```
1   prepare the pack
2   choose a dealer
3   prepare the pack
4   deal the cards
5   sort the hands
```

Figure 2.1

Notice that steps 1 and 3 are identical; the reason why will become apparent as we refine the design.

We have already hinted that we would prepare the pack for dealing by initializing the array *pack*. The simulation of shuffling the pack and the resulting random appearance of the cards in the deal will be considered in the design of steps 2 and 4. The refinement of step 1 would be

```
1.1   initialize the array pack
```

and this could be done using a loop.

2.2 Choosing a dealer

There are several ways of choosing a dealer; in step 2 we shall use the method which is sometimes called 'first jack up'. This method involves dealing a card to each player in turn, face up, repeating the cycle until the first jack is dealt. The 'dealer to be' is the player who receives this first jack.

The refinement of step 2, 'choose a dealer', could then be written as in Figure 2.2.

```
2.1   deal a card to the first player
2.2   loop while last card dealt is not a jack
2.3      deal a card to the next player in rotation
2.4   loopend
2.5   the last player to be dealt a card is the dealer
2.6   write out the identity of the dealer
```

Figure 2.2

There are a number of steps that need further refinement and the problems that immediately appear to need attention are:

(i) How do we identify the first player to receive a card and each of the players?

(ii) How do we simulate a deal with its requirement of randomness?

The solution to the first problem is somewhat arbitrary; we declare a variable, say *player* to represent the player to receive the card to be dealt and the type of the variable may be chosen to accommodate whatever values we decide to use to identify the individual players. Of course the values used must all be of the same type.

SAQ 2.1

For each of the following sets of values which may be used to identify the players, specify the Pascal type you would choose for the variable *player*

(i) Eddie, Hilda, Pauline, David

(ii) A, B, C, D

(iii) player1, player2, player3, player4

(iv) 1, 2, 3, 4

Solution 2.1

(i) *string* or *string*[7]. if the second option is chosen the maximum length of the string which is specified must be large enough to allow all of the names to be assigned. Thus, in this case since the longest name, Pauline, has seven characters the specified maximum string size must be at least seven.

(ii) *char*. If you have specified *string* your answer is not incorrect but it will result in a wasteful use of storage.

(iii) *string* or *string*[7]. Again the second alternative will result in a more economic use of storage. Note that 1, 2, 3, 4 as used in these values are *characters* and not integers, so for instance if *player* = *player2* the Pascal statement

```
player = player + 1
```

will not assign the value *player3* to *player*, but will in fact produce a syntax error since an integer cannot be added to a string.

(iv) *integer*.

For convenience of manipulation and generality we shall use the integers 1, 2, 3, 4 to represent the four players, so the variable *player* would be declared to be of type *integer*.

To simulate the deal, which in effect involves a random selection of cards from the pack, we shall use a random number generator which produces a random number in the range 1..52. This random number generator is appropriately called *random* and the Pascal statement

```
card := random
```

will result in the integer variable *card* being assigned an integer value in the specified range. Since we have represented the cards in the pack by the integers 1 to 52 the above process, in effect, randomly selects a card from the pack. This card may then be allocated to a player. The fact that the card has been dealt, and is therefore no longer in the pack, is recorded by setting the appropriate element of the array *pack* to *false*.

A refinement of step 2.1 would then be as shown in Figure 2.3.

```
2.1.1   initialize player
2.1.2   generate an integer, card, using random
2.1.3   remove card from pack
```

Figure 2.3

Step 2.2 of Figure 2.2 requires only a minor refinement: identifying the numbers of the cards which are jacks.

SAQ 2.2

State the four integers in the range 1 to 52 which represent a jack.

Solution 2.2
11, 24, 37, 50

The refinement of step 2.2 is thus

```
2.2.1   loop while card is not one of 11, 24, 37, 50
```

Let us now consider step 2.3, 'deal a card to the next player in rotation'. Before we can implement the deal we need to identify the next player in rotation. It is reasonable to specify that cards are dealt to players in player order

..1, 2, 3, 4, 1, 2, 3, 4, 1, 2, 3, 4, 1, ..., etc.

Consequently, since *player* is an *integer* variable, the next player would be identified by adding 1 to the current value of *player*

unless the current value is 4 when the next player would be 1. The refinement of 2.3 would then begin as shown in Figure 2.4.

```
2.3.1   if player = 4
2.3.2   then
2.3.3       set player to 1
2.3.4   else
2.3.5       set player to player + 1
2.3.6   ifend
```

Figure 2.4

Note that if *player* was not of type *integer* this step would not be so easily implemented. Also, as we are only interested in determining who is to be the dealer, there is no need to remember which cards go to which player. (We only need to record the fact that the card has been removed from the pack.)

SAQ 2.3

Before proceeding, consider the implementation of the deal in step 2.3 of Figure 2.2 and compare the situation with that in step 2.1 of Figure 2.2. Are there any considerations that need to be taken into account in step 2.3 that were not necessary in step 2.1?

Solution 2.3

In step 2.1 since no cards had been removed the number produced by *random* always identified a card that is contained in the pack. However, when step 2.3 is executed cards will have been removed. When the step is executed for the first time one card will have been removed and the more times it is executed the more cards will be missing from the pack. Consequently in step 2.3 it is possible for *random* to generate an integer which represents a card that has been removed already.

The design which constitutes the complete refinement of step 2.3 must therefore contain a strategy which caters for this possible complication. At this stage we shall use the simplest method, which is to generate integers repeatedly until one occurs that represents a card that is still in the pack. You may well realize that this is not the most efficient way, but its simplicity is helpful at this stage. To ascertain whether or not this is the case the element of the array *pack*, indexed by the integer generated, is tested. If the value of the element is *false* the card has been dealt. The refinement which implements the strategy is shown in Figure 2.5.

```
2.3.7    generate an integer, card, using random
2.3.8    loop while pack[card] is false
2.3.9      generate an integer, card, using random
2.3.10   loopend
2.3.11   remove card from the pack
```

Figure 2.5

Step 2.5 can now be refined to 2.5.1 using a variable *dealer* of the same type as player. Similarly, step 2.6 can be refined to 2.6.1 so that the contents of the variable *dealer* are written out.

The complete refinement of steps 1 and 2 of our top-level design are now as shown in Figure 2.6.

```
1.1      initialize the array pack
2.1.1    initialize player
2.1.2    generate an integer card using random
2.1.3    remove card from pack
2.2.1    loop while card is not one of 11, 24, 37, 50
2.3.1      if player = 4
2.3.2      then
2.3.3        set player to 1
2.3.4      else
2.3.5        set player to player + 1
2.3.6      ifend
2.3.7      generate an integer card using random
2.3.8      loop while pack[card] is false
2.3.9        generate an integer card using random
2.3.10     loopend
2.3.11     remove card from pack
2.4      loopend
2.5.1    set the value of dealer to the value of player
2.6.1    write out dealer
```

Figure 2.6 *The design to choose a dealer*

Exercise 2.1 _____

Complete the data table in Figure 2.7 for the design in Figure 2.6.

Identifier	Description	Type
player dealer card k pack	loop control variable for step 1.1	

Figure 2.7

(Note: the random number generator *random* may be ignored for this exercise since it is not a variable; its inclusion in the program will be achieved by using a Pascal unit. The program text will require a **uses** statement which will be provided by the Course Team.)

2.3 Dealing and sorting the hands

Having chosen the dealer, before we can begin the deal, we need to collect in the cards and, again, prepare the pack for dealing. This is step 3 of our top-level design shown in Figure 2.1, which, like step 1, involves setting all the elements of the array *pack* to *true*. This is expressed in design terms as:

```
3.1    initialize the array pack
```

We are now ready to begin our task of dealing the hands. We have already indicated that we are assuming that there are four players and now we shall further specify that we wish to deal 28 cards so that each player has a hand of seven cards. We thus need to simulate a deal of one card to each of the four players and repeat this process seven times. The first player to receive a card is the player who 'follows' the dealer in the sequence 1, 2, 3, 4, 1, ...

SAQ 2.4 _____

For the following selections of dealer, state the number of the player who would receive the first card in the deal.

(i) dealer is player number 2

(ii) dealer is player number 4

Solution 2.4

The first player to receive a card in the deal would be:

(i) player number 3

(ii) player number 1

A strategy to implement the deal would be as shown in Figure 2.8.

```
4.1    loop for seven rounds
4.2      deal a card to each of the four players
4.3    loopend
4.4    write out the contents of each hand
```

Figure 2.8

Before we can model the deal we must have some structure to represent 'a hand'. The structure we shall use is an *array*. We shall represent each of the four hands by an *array* of *seven elements*; each element being an integer in the range 1..52 representing the particular card dealt. Suppose we call the four arrays *hand1, hand2, hand3, hand4* representing the hands of players 1, 2, 3 and 4 respectively.

Thus, the implementation of step 4.2 can be refined as shown in Figure 2.9.

4.2.1	loop for the number of players
4.2.2	identify the player to receive the card
4.2.3	deal a card
4.2.4	insert it in the player's hand
4.2.5	loopend

Figure 2.9

Step 4.2.2 involves identifying the next player in the player cycle starting with the player following the dealer. We have already done a similar refinement in steps 2.3.1 to 2.3.6 of Figure 2.6.

Step 4.2.3 is the deal itself as in steps 2.3.7 to 2.3.11 of Figure 2.6. The final step involves the selection of the correct hand before insertion of the card. Note that we shall insert the card dealt to each player in the first round of the deal in location 1 of the appropriate array (hand), the card dealt in the second round is inserted in location 2 and so on.

SAQ 2.5

Write down the element of the array which holds each of the following cards:

(i) The card dealt to player number 4 in the first round of the deal.

(ii) The card dealt to player number 1 in the sixth round of the deal.

Solution 2.5
(i) *hand4[1]* (ii) *hand1[6]*

The appropriate hand would be located using a *nested-if* construction involving the arrangement of steps shown in Figure 2.10.

We continue the refinement in this way up to step 4.2.4.16 as you will see in Figure 2.11.

Implementing each of the three stages and combining them together in a loop executed four times (as there are four players), gives the refinement of step 4.2 shown in Figure 2.11.

If we now combine Figure 2.8 and 2.11 we have a refinement of our original step 4.

To summarize our present position:

We have chosen a dealer—the design is shown in Figure 2.6

4.2.4.1	if player = 1
4.2.4.2	then
4.2.4.3	set appropriate element of hand1 to card
4.2.4.4	else
4.2.4.5	if player = 2
4.2.4.6	then ...

Figure 2.10

4.2.1.1	loop for four repetitions
4.2.2.1	if player = 4
4.2.2.2	then
4.2.2.3	set player to 1
4.2.2.4	else
4.2.2.5	set player to player + 1
4.2.2.6	ifend
4.2.3.1	generate an integer card using random
4.2.3.2	loop while pack[card] is false
4.2.3.3	generate an integer card using random
4.2.3.4	loopend
4.2.3.5	remove card from pack
4.2.4.1	if player = 1
4.2.4.2	then
4.2.4.3	set appropriate element of hand1 to card
4.2.4.4	else
4.2.4.5	if player = 2
4.2.4.6	then
4.2.4.7	set appropriate element of hand2 to card
4.2.4.8	else
4.2.4.9	if player = 3
4.2.4.10	then
4.2.4.11	set appropriate element of hand3 to card
4.2.4.12	else
4.2.4.13	set appropriate element of hand4 to card
4.2.4.14	ifend
4.2.4.15	ifend
4.2.4.16	ifend
4.2.5	loopend

Figure 2.11 *Select hand and insert card*

We have dealt four hands, each of seven cards—the design is shown in Figures 2.8 and 2.11.

By combining all these designs—Figures 2.6, 2.8, 2.11 and 2.1—we get the complete design shown in Figure 2.12 and the data table in Figure 2.13.

At this stage the cards in the hands are in random order, and we have four arrays *hand1*, *hand2*, *hand3* and *hand4* each containing seven unordered integer elements. Remember, each integer is in the range 1 to 52 and uniquely represents a card in the pack. The only task that now remains, step 5 of our top-level design in

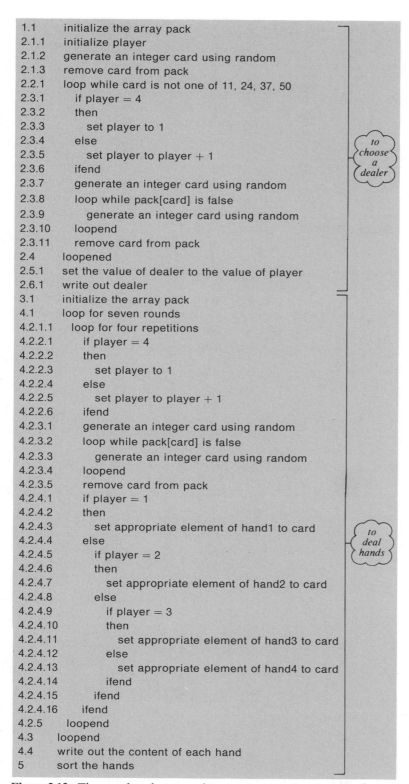

```
1.1       initialize the array pack
2.1.1     initialize player
2.1.2     generate an integer card using random
2.1.3     remove card from pack
2.2.1     loop while card is not one of 11, 24, 37, 50
2.3.1        if player = 4
2.3.2        then
2.3.3           set player to 1
2.3.4        else
2.3.5           set player to player + 1
2.3.6        ifend
2.3.7        generate an integer card using random
2.3.8        loop while pack[card] is false
2.3.9           generate an integer card using random
2.3.10       loopend
2.3.11       remove card from pack
2.4       loopened
2.5.1     set the value of dealer to the value of player
2.6.1     write out dealer
3.1       initialize the array pack
4.1       loop for seven rounds
4.2.1.1      loop for four repetitions
4.2.2.1         if player = 4
4.2.2.2         then
4.2.2.3            set player to 1
4.2.2.4         else
4.2.2.5            set player to player + 1
4.2.2.6         ifend
4.2.3.1         generate an integer card using random
4.2.3.2         loop while pack[card] is false
4.2.3.3            generate an integer card using random
4.2.3.4         loopend
4.2.3.5         remove card from pack
4.2.4.1         if player = 1
4.2.4.2         then
4.2.4.3            set appropriate element of hand1 to card
4.2.4.4         else
4.2.4.5            if player = 2
4.2.4.6            then
4.2.4.7               set appropriate element of hand2 to card
4.2.4.8            else
4.2.4.9               if player = 3
4.2.4.10              then
4.2.4.11                 set appropriate element of hand3 to card
4.2.4.12              else
4.2.4.13                 set appropriate element of hand4 to card
4.2.4.14              ifend
4.2.4.15           ifend
4.2.4.16        ifend
4.2.5        loopend
4.3       loopend
4.4       write out the content of each hand
5         sort the hands
```

Figure 2.12 *The complete design to choose a dealer and to deal hands*

Identifier	Description	Type
player	identity of player receiving next card	integer variable
dealer	identity of dealer	integer variable
round	number of dealing round—control variable for outer for loop	integer variable
repetition	control variable for inner for loop	integer variable
pack	array representing a pack of cards showing cards remaining in the pack	array [1..52] of Boolean variable
hand1	representation of hand of player number 1	array [1..7] of integer variable
hand2	representation of hand of player number 2	array [1..7] of integer variable
hand3	representation of hand of player number 3	array [1..7] of integer variable
hand4	representation of hand of player number 4	array [1..7] of integer variable
card	variable to which output of random number generator is assigned	integer variable
k	control variable for pack initialization for loop	integer variable

Figure 2.13 *The complete data table for the design as shown in Figure 2.12*

2.4 Implementing the design in Pascal

In this section we shall begin to implement in Pascal part of the design we have just developed.

Let us begin the implementation by focusing our attention only on the part of the design that chooses the dealer. You will, therefore, need to refer to Figure 2.6 and to the associated data table in Figure 2.7 for the remainder of this section.

Exercise 2.2 _____

Refer to the data table in the solution to Exercise 2.1 and write the **type** and **var** sections of the program.

Figure 2.1, is to sort the hands. This could be done using the selection sort method described in *Unit II.2*, but we will not refine this step further.

Exercise 2.3 _____

Given the declarations in Exercise 2.2 write a program segment to implement step 1.1 of the design.

If we now assume that player number 1 is to be the first player to receive a card, steps 2.1.1 to 2.1.3 will result in the following code:

```
player:= 1;
card:= random;
pack[card]:= false;
```

The **while** loop which begins at step 2.2.1 and ends at step 2.4 involves a condition using *Boolean* operations which we shall treat in depth in Section 4 of this unit. So, for the moment we shall simply state the **while** statement that will implement the required action:

while not ((card = 11) **or** (card = 24) **or** (card = 37) **or** (card = 50)) **do**

The complete program, *choosedealer*, is shown in Figure 2.14. Notice again the strategy within the **while** loop:

1 Select the next player to receive a card (the **if** statement).

```
program choosedealer;
uses {$u udealer.code} udealer;
type cardarray = array[1..52] of Boolean;
var
   player, card, k: integer;
   pack: cardarray;
begin
   {initialize the array pack}
   for k:= 1 to 52 do
      pack[k]:= true;
   {select first player and deal a card}
   player:= 1;
   card:= random;
   pack[card]:= false;
   {continue deal until first jack appears}
   while not ((card = 11) or (card = 24) or (card = 37) or (card = 50)) do
      begin
         {select next player to receive a card}
         if player = 4
         then
            player:= 1
         else
            player:= player + 1;
         {deal a card}
         card:= random;
         while pack[card] = false do
            card:= random;
            pack[card]:= false
      end;
   writeln;
   writeln('The dealer is player number ', player)
end.
```

Figure 2.14 *The choosedealer program*

2 Repeatedly generate an integer using *random* until a card is identified that is still in the pack.

The second stage is achieved using a **while** loop and the array *pack* is not updated until we exit from this loop, i.e. until we have actually dealt a card.

Note that *random*, as used in the program *choosedealer*, is contained in the *unit* called *udealer* which is named in the **uses** statement. Notice also that we have written out *player* instead of assigning it to *dealer*. Hence, *dealer* is redundant, so it is not used in the program.

Practical exercise 2.1 _____

The purpose of this exercise is to give you some experience of the program *choosedealer* and to give you a copy of the program which we shall ask you to modify later in the unit.

(i)   Transfer the following files to your user disk:
      B2:UDEALER.CODE
      B2:DDEALER.TEXT
      B2:PDEALER.TEXT
      The last of these files contains the program *choosedealer* and the second is a data file used by *random*.

(ii) Compile and run the program *choosedealer*.

(iii) Modify the program to enable you to see the integers generated by *random* and the integer identifying the eventual card dealt. Run the modified program.

(iv) You may wish to save a copy of the modified program.

(v)   You may find it useful to have a listing of *choosedealer* to refer to later in the unit.

2.5 Summary of section

We began this section by introducing the problem of simulating a game of cards. In particular we concentrated on the stages that comprise the preparation phase, developing program designs for two of the stages identified, and took one design as far as the implementation in Pascal.

The program designs we have developed in this section have used both **while** and **for** loops; in the next section we introduce a third looping construct.

3 *Loops*

3.1 Pre and postconditioned loops

The loops you have met so far in the course and which we used in the previous section (the **for** loop and the **while** loop) may be classified by the strategy used to control the number of repetitions of the loop. In the **for** loop the number of repetitions is determined when the program is executed by the initial and final values of the control variable. The **while** loop, on the other hand, is an example of the **dynamic** control of a loop. In this case the number of times the loop statements are executed is determined at execution time by the results of the processing within the loop; there are no control variables.

The **while** loop is called a **preconditioned** loop because the test condition is evaluated *before* the loop is executed. In the design language we express such as loop as

```
loop condition
    actions to be performed
loopend
```

The test condition can, alternatively, be placed *after* the actions, in which case we have a **postconditioned** loop

```
loop
    actions to be performed
loopend condition
```

A *postconditioned* loop is written in the program design language as

```
loop
    actions to be performed
until condition
loopend
```

In the postconditioned loop construct the actions are as follows:

(i) The statements between *loop* and *until* are executed.

(ii) The condition is evaluated and if the condition is *false* steps (i) and (ii) are repeated. If the condition is *true* control passes to the next statement in sequence.

Thus, the loop is successively executed until the condition is satisfied. This latter loop is often referred to as a *repeat-until* loop.

SAQ 3.1

Classify each of the following two loops as preconditioned or postconditioned.

(i)

```
1.1   loop while there are invoices to be processed
1.2       process an invoice
1.3   loopend
```

(ii)

```
1.1   loop
1.2       read in a number
1.3       update the total using the number
1.4   until there are no more numbers
1.5   loopend
```

Solution 3.1

(i) is a preconditioned loop

(ii) is a postconditioned loop

In a *preconditioned* loop the condition is tested *before* the loop is executed. In a *postconditioned* loop the condition is tested *after* the loop is executed. As a consequence of this, it is possible in certain circumstances for a preconditioned loop not to be executed at all.

In the postconditioned loop, since the terminating condition is tested *after* the loop is executed, the earliest opportunity to stop the execution of the loop occurs at the end of the first loop cycle. Thus, a postconditioned loop must be executed at least once.

SAQ 3.2

Under what circumstances will a preconditioned loop not be executed at all?

Solution 3.2

When the *while* condition is *false* at the time that the loop is met for the first time.

Consider the 'choose a dealer' problem again, which is reproduced in Figure 3.1.

1.1	initialize the array pack
2.1.1	initialize player
2.1.2	generate an integer card using random
2.1.3	remove card from pack
2.2.1	loop while card is not one of 11, 24, 37, 50
2.3.1	if player = 4
2.3.2	then
2.3.3	set player to 1
2.3.4	else
2.3.5	set player to player + 1
2.3.6	ifend
2.3.7	generate an integer card using random
2.3.8	loop while pack[card] is false
2.3.9	generate an integer card using random
2.3.10	loopend
2.3.11	remove card from pack
2.4	loopend
2.5.1	set the value of dealer to the value of player
2.6.1	write out dealer

Figure 3.1 *The design to choose a dealer*

In step 2.2.1 of this design if card has the value 11 or 24 or 37 or 54 then the condition is false so steps 2.3.1 to 2.3.11 are not executed, that is the loop will not be executed at all.

Exercise 3.1 _____

Rewrite steps 2.3.7 to 2.3.10, the 'deal a card' segment of the design in Figure 3.1, as a postconditioned loop.

Exercise 3.2 _____

A program is required to produce a graphical representation of data. The program is to read in a sequence of non-negative integers; there is always at least one number in the sequence. For each integer input the program is to write out a row of asterisks, the number of asterisks being determined by the integer input. The input sequence is terminated by a sentinel, a negative integer which, of course, is not to be processed. For example the sequence 2, 10, 0, 3, −4 would result in the output in Figure 3.2.

```
* *

* * * * * * * * * *

* * *
```

Figure 3.2

Produce two top-level designs for such a program. Your solutions are to use:

(i) a *preconditioned* loop
(ii) a *postconditioned* loop

3.2 The anatomy of conditioned loops (Tape section)

Before studying this section find the audio cassette for this unit.

Each frame in the text is discussed on the tape. A jingle will indicate when you should stop the tape.

Frame 1

Two points to look for:

Point 1: Variables which are updated inside any loop may need to be initialized *prior* to *entering* the loop.

Point 2: Any variables used in the condition (i.e. the test) part of a *preconditioned* loop. These variables, also, must be initialized *prior* to *entering* the loop.

Frame 2

A set of positive integers, terminated by a zero, is to be input and summed. The sum is to be output.

Solution A	Solution B
1 set sum to zero	1 set sum to zero
2 read in value	2 loop
3 loop while value is not zero	3 read in value
4 add value to sum	4 add value to sum
5 read in value	5 until value is zero
6 loopend	6 loopend
7 write out sum	7 write out sum

Frame 3

A set of non-negative integers, terminated by a negative integer, is to be input and summed. The sum is to be output.

Frame 4

Solution A	Solution B
1 set sum to zero	1 set sum to zero
2 read in value	2 loop
3 loop while value is non-negative	3 read in value
4 add value to sum	4 add value to sum
5 read in value	5 until value is negative
6 loopend	6 loopend
7 write out sum	7 write out sum

Frame 5

3 4 0 10 −5

Frame 6

Step	Variables		Condition
executed	*sum*	*value*	'*value* is negative'
1	0		
3		3	
4	3		
5			false
3		4	
4	7		
5			false
3		0	
4	7		
5			false

Frame 7

```
1   set sum to zero
2   read in value
3   loop
4       add value to sum
5       read in value
6   until value is negative
7   loopend
8   write out sum
```

Frame 8

In a *postconditioned* loop it may or may not be necessary to initialize *loop condition variables*—the choice of action depends on the context.

Frame 9

The array is indexed from zero to 100 and the locations with indexes 1 to *size* have valid elements.

```
1   initialize updated variables
2   loop
3       decrement index
4   until array[index] = required value
5   loopend
```

Frame 10

```
1   loop
2       ask user if another search is required (Y or N)
3       input response
4   until response = 'Y' or 'N'
5   loopend
```

Frame 11

```
1   initialize sum to zero
2   initialize count to one
3   loop
4       increment sum by count
5       increment count
6   until count = 11
7   loopend
```

Frame 12

```
1   initialize sum to zero
2   initialize count to zero
3   loop
4       increment count
5       increment sum by count
6   until count = 10
7   loopend
```

Frame 13

```
1   initialize sum to zero
2   initialize count to one
3   loop while count <= 10
4       increment sum by count
5       increment count
6   loopend
```

Frame 14

```
1   initialize sum to zero
2   initialize count to one
3   loop
4       increment sum by 1/count
5       double the value of count
6   until sum > 2
7   loopend
```

Frame 15

Rules to be observed when using conditioned loops:

1 All variables updated inside the loop must be initialized prior to entering the loop.

2 There must be at least one statement within the loop which has an effect on the variable(s) in the termination condition.

3 The condition affecting termination of the loop must eventually be satisfied.

4 When using a preconditioned loop any variable used in the condition must be initialized.

3.3 Pre and postconditioned loops in Pascal

You have already had experience of preconditioned loops and written programs implementing them as **while** loops.

In this section we will look at *postconditioned* loops and how they are implemented in Pascal as **repeat until** loops;

```
repeat
    statement(s)
until condition
```

The statements to be executed repeatedly are written between the reserved words **repeat** and **until** and separated by semicolons. The **repeat until** construct does not require the use of **begin** and **end** to group statements together. The reserved words **repeat** and **until** themselves fulfil this function.

As an example consider the program in Figure 3.3.

```
sum:= 0;
repeat
    write('enter a number ');
    readln(number);
    sum:= sum + number
until sum > 1000;
```

Figure 3.3

The program reads numbers and sums them until the sum is greater than 1000. The condition *sum > 1000* and the statements within the loop are executed *until* the condition becomes *true*. Note that, in a **repeat until** loop the condition is evaluated *after* the statements are executed. Remember also that each statement within the loop *except the last one* is separated from the preceding statement by a *semicolon*.

SAQ 3.3

Look at the program in Figure 3.4 and state what the output will be when the program is run.

```
program posttest;
var
    number: integer;
begin
    number:= 19;
    repeat
        writeln(number);
        number:= number - 1
    until number = 8
end.
```

Figure 3.4

Solution 3.3

The output will be a list of integers from 19 down to 9.

Note that *number* is initialized to 19 and on the first pass through the loop this value is written out. The terminating condition for the loop is *number = 8* since *number* is decremented by 1 after each write statement and we want to stop after the value 9 is output. An alternative program would include the loop shown in Figure 3.5.

```
number:= 20;
repeat
    number:= number - 1;
    writeln(number)
until number = 9
```

Figure 3.5

Practical exercise 3.1 _____

In Practical exercise 3.1 in *Unit 1* of this block you were asked to write the body of a program called *linear1* which performed a linear search on an array called *ladder*. Find your solution to this activity or obtain the solution from the block disk **B2:ALINEAR1.TEXT** and modify the program so that a postconditioned loop is used for the search instead of a preconditioned loop. Call your modified program *postlinear*. Run *postlinear* and locate the position of the name *Boyd* in the array *ladder*.

Before starting this practical exercise you will have to make copies of the following programs on your user disk:

B2:ALINEAR1.TEXT
B2:ULINEAR1.CODE

When you run your program the input *Boyd* should give the output:

Name found at index 6

3.4 The for loop

So far in this section we have devoted our time to the study of loops in which the number of repetitions of the loop is controlled by the results of the execution of the statements within the loop. We have also used another kind of loop control, in which the number of repetitions is determined at execution time, before the loop is entered. This is the **for** loop or **for to** loop. To complete our discussion of looping we shall introduce you to the **for downto** loop.

You will remember that a **for** loop uses a control variable which is incremented on each execution of the loop. The **for downto** statement is executed in a similar manner to the **for to** loop but after each pass through the loop the index is *decremented* by 1. For example:

```
for i := 50 downto 2 do
    A[i] := A[i − 1]
```

(where A: **array** [1..50] **of** integer)

This loop copies A[49] into A[50], A[48] into A[49] and so on. The index variable, i, takes the values 50, 49, 48...2. However, consider:

```
for i := 38 downto 40 do
    A[i] := A[i − 1]
```

In this case the **for** loop is not executed, because 40, the final value, is greater than 38, the initial value.

Exercise 3.3 _____

The array parts is declared as *parts: **array**[1..50] **of** string*. This array currently holds the names of 40 items and this value is held in the variable *stockitems*. The array is sorted so that the elements are in alphabetical order. We wish to insert a new item, the value of the *string* variable *newe1*. The situation is that we have performed a linear or binary search, as described in the previous unit, and have discovered that items in locations 1 to 16 precede the new item alphabetically and items in locations 17 to 40 are greater (alphabetically speaking) than the new item. Assuming that we have already confirmed that the array has space for the new item:

(i) List the three tasks we need to perform to insert the new item.

(ii) Write a program segment that will implement these tasks, using a **for downto** statement.

3.5 Summary of section

In this section we analysed the three techniques that we now have for achieving repetition. The **for** statement is a construct where the number of repetitions is determined at execution time, whereas the **while** and **repeat** statements enable dynamic control of the number of repetitions to be achieved. We described the syntax of the repeat statement in Pascal and compared the **while** and **repeat** statements, introducing the terms *preconditioned* and *postconditioned* to describe their respective control strategies. To complete the trio of statements for controlling repetition we summarized the operational details of the **for to** and **for downto** statements.

4 *Conditions*

4.1 Introduction

As we have progressed through the course we have used tests involving conditions in both design steps and program statements. These have ranged from statements such as **if** *character = space* in *Block I* and **while** *grade < > −1* in *Unit 1* of this block, to statements involving more complicated conditions such as **while** *number of passes is less than n − 1* in the previous unit. Finally, you met the statement **while not** ((*card = 11*) **or** (*card = 24*) **or** (*card = 37*) **or** (*card = 50*)) in the *choosedealer* program. Each time we have introduced such a test we have justified it in the context in which it was used, but apart from a short piece in *Unit 3* of *Block I* we have not discussed this important topic in isolation. However, in this section we shall look in detail at conditions as separate entities and formalize the intuitive ideas with which you have become familiar.

4.2 Simple conditions

A *condition* is an expression which has the value *true* or *false*. Thus, it is often referred to as a *Boolean* expression.

SAQ 4.1 _____

If the integer variables *count* and *total* have the values 12 and 50 respectively and the character variable *item* has the value *'x'* what are the values of the following conditions, *true* or *false*?

(i) count < 15	(ii) count + 1 < > total
(iii) item = 'X'	(iv) total = count ∗ 4 + 2

Solution 4.1

(i), (ii) and (iv) are *true*.

(iii) is *false* (an upper case character is not equal to a lower case character).

The symbols '<', '<>', '=' used in the SAQ examples are called **comparison operators**. The following comparison operators are available in Pascal:

=	'is equal to'
< >	'is not equal to'
<	'is less than'
< =	'is less than or equal to'
> =	'is greater than or equal to'
>	'is greater than'

Figure 4.1

All of these operators may be used to compare expressions of type *real*, *integer*, *character*, *Boolean* and *string*. (An expression may consist of just one variable or constant.) The essential feature is that the expression occurring on the *left*-hand side of the operator *must* be of the same type as that occurring on the *right*-hand side.

SAQ 4.2 _____

Assuming that *breadth*, *depth* and *size* are *integer* variables, *initial* and *class* are *character* variables and *flag* is a *Boolean* variable, which of the following expressions are acceptable conditions?

(i)	breadth < 12	(ii)	size = class
(iii)	depth > = 20	(iv)	flag < > false
(v)	flag = 'true'	(vi)	initial > 'J'
(vii)	class = '2'	(viii)	size = breadth ∗ depth
(ix)	class = 4		

Solution 4.2

(i), (iii), (iv), (vi), (vii) and (viii) are acceptable.

(ii) is invalid: an *integer* is being compared with a *character*

(v) is invalid: a *Boolean* quantity is being compared with a *string*

(ix) is invalid: a *character* is being compared with an *integer* (note that 4 is an *integer*, '4' is a *character*)

The comparison illustrated in part (vi) may be intuitively acceptable, but consider *initial > ';'*. This comparison too is a valid one and, in fact, if *initial* is an alphabetic *character* the result of this comparison is *true*. The condition is evaluated by comparing the ASCII codes of the items concerned. Each character of type *char* has an ASCII code. The code for the character

';' is less than the code for any alphabetic character. Also, upper case characters precede lower case characters so that $'X' < 'a'$ is *true*. *Strings* are compared character by character so that $'apple' < 'Ball'$ is *false*.

4.3 The Boolean operators and compound conditions

We often wish to construct conditions which involve more than a single comparison. The operators **and, or** and **not** enable us to construct a condition of any complexity.

The operator **and** takes two *Boolean* operands and gives a Boolean result which has the value *true* if and only if *both* operands are *true*. Thus

    (count < 10) and (sum <= 100)

is true if *both* the variable *count* has a value less than *10* and the variable *sum* has a value less than, or equal to *100*. It is *false* otherwise, i.e. if one or both of the operands are false. Notice the necessity for *brackets*, all three Boolean operators **and, or** and **not** have precedence over the comparison operators listed in Figure 4.1. The brackets ensure that the conditions are evaluated before the **and** operation takes place. As in ordinary arithmetic, there are rules such as *multiplication* and *division* taking precedence over *addition* and *subtraction*, so in Pascal there are strict rules of precedence that govern the evaluation of expressions. We shall not consider all of these rules in detail; instead we shall rely on the insertion of brackets to ensure that the expressions are evaluated as we intend.

SAQ 4.3

What is the value of
(count < 10) **and** (sum <= 100) if

(i)   count = 10, sum = 50
(ii) count = 20, sum = 200
(iii) count = 4, sum = 40
(iv) count = 9, sum = 110

Solution 4.3
(i) false   (ii) false   (iii) true   (iv) false

The operator **or** also takes two *Boolean* operands and yields a *Boolean* result which has the value *true* if *one* or *both* of the operands are *true*; it has the value *false* if and *only* if both operands have the value *false*. Thus

    (count < 10) or (sum <= 100)

has the value *true* if either *count* has a value less than *10* or *sum* has a value less than or equal to *100*; alternatively both conditions may be *true*.

SAQ 4.4

What is the value of
(count < 10) **or** (sum <= 100) if

(i)   count = 10, sum = 100
(ii) count = 20, sum = 700
(iii) count = 5, sum = 20
(iv) count = 7, sum = 210

Solution 4.4
(i) true   (ii) false   (iii) true   (iv) true

We say that **and** and **or** are *binary* operators because they require two operands. The operator **not** is *unary*; it takes a single *Boolean* operand and yields a *Boolean* result. For example:

> If the Boolean variable *found* has the value *true*, then **not** *found* has the value *false*.
> If *found* has the value *false* then **not** *found* has the value *true*.

SAQ 4.5

In the program, *choosedealer* the following statement appeared:

    while pack[card] = false do
       card := random;

Rewrite this statement using the operator **not** in the condition.

Solution 4.5

    while not pack[card] = true do
       card := random;

The statement *card := random* is repeated as long as the condition *pack[card]* = *false* is true. If *pack[card]* is false then **not** *pack[card]* is true, and so **not** *pack[card]* = *true* is true and the two conditions are equivalent.

The results just described may be expressed in a table as shown in Figures 4.2 and 4.3.

x and y are *Boolean* terms or expressions.

x	y	x **and** y	x **or** y		x	**not** x
true	true	true	true		true	false
true	false	false	true		false	true
false	true	false	true			
false	false	false	false			

Figure 4.2   **Figure 4.3**

These tables for the evaluation of *Boolean* expressions are called **truth tables**.

Exercise 4.1 _____

If *number* and *total* are integer variables, *maxval* is an integer constant, *success* is a Boolean variable and *colour* is a character variable, determine the ranges of values that will cause the following Boolean expressions to yield the value *true*.

(i)   (*number* > 4) **and** (*total* >= 100)
(ii) (*colour* = 'r') **or** (*colour* = 'w')
(iii) (**not** *success*) **or** (*number* < *maxval*)
(iv) ((*number* > 0) **and** (*number* < 10)) **or** *success*
(v)   (**not** (*number* < 20)) **and** (*number* > 10)
(vi) (**not** (*number* < 20)) **and** (*number* < 10)

As we have already indicated the priority of evaluation in a complex expression can appear a complicated business. The 'golden rule' is *if in doubt put in brackets*. In fact **not** has the highest priority of *all* operators in Pascal followed by **and** and then **or**. The relative priority of the three Boolean operators is:

not
and
or

so that in part (iii) of Exercise 4.1:
We did not need the brackets around **not** *success*. Since **not** is evaluated before **or** the expression

not *success* **or** (*number* < *maxval*)

would have achieved the required effect. In part (iv) since **and** has a higher priority than **or** the expression could have been written without bracketing the **and** part, that is as

(*number* > 0) **and** (*number* < 10) **or** *success*

In part (v) the brackets around the first condition are not necessary, i.e. **not** (*number* < 20) **and** (*number* > 10) is adequate. A similar comment applies to part (vi); the brackets around the first condition are not necessary.

However, as you can see from these four examples it is good practice to use brackets to ensure that the order of evaluation intended is carried out. As an added bonus, the use of brackets often adds to the clarity of the statement.

Exercise 4.2 _____

Write down Boolean expressions which will yield the value true if

(i)   the integer variable *month* has a value between 1 and 12 inclusive
(ii) the string variable *answer* has either the value '*y*' or '*yes*'
(iii) the Boolean variable *stop* is *false* and the integer variable *index* > *start* where *start* is an integer constant
(iv) the integer variable *ordertotal* is greater than 12 or the string variable *city* is not equal to the string variable *location* or the string variable *depot*.

Exercise 4.3 _____

(i)   *number* is an integer variable. *positive*, *zero* and *negative* are Boolean variables. Write a segment of program that will set *positive* to *true* if *number* is greater than zero, *zero* to *true* if *number* is equal to zero, and *negative* to *true* if *number* is less than *zero*. In each case the other variables are set to *false*.

(ii) *day* and *month* are integer variables and *datevalid* is a Boolean variable. Write a segment of program that will result in *datevalid* being set to true if *month* is equal to 1 and *day* is in the range 1 to 31 inclusive and *false* otherwise.

As a further example, suppose we wish to determine whether or not a particular person is a member of some organization. An array *members* holds the names of all the members of the organization. *members* is declared as an array with elements of type *string* with an index range *1..limit*, where *limit* is an integer constant. At any time *members* holds a name in locations *1..size* where *size* is an integer variable.

Suppose now that the string variable *person* holds the name of the individual in question and *isamember* is a *Boolean* variable. Consider the following program segment:

```
index := size + 1;
repeat
    index := index − 1;
    isamember := (members[index] = person)
until isamember or (index = 1)
```

Figure 4.4

This program segment implements a linear search, which terminates when the whole of the array currently in use has been searched or when the person under investigation has been located in the array. At the end of the search the value of *isamember* indicates whether or not the individual is a member of the organization. The statement

isamember: = (members[index] = person)

causes the variable *isamember* to be assigned the value *true* if members[index] = person and the value *false* otherwise.

Exercise 4.4

(i) If the date of my birthday is 16th November, write an assignment statement that will cause the appropriate value to be assigned to the Boolean variable *ismybirthday* if the integer variables *day* and *month* specify the current date.

(ii) A job advertisement specifies that, to be eligible for appointment, an applicant must be between the ages of 25 and 35 (inclusive) and be unmarried. If the integer variable *age* and the Boolean variable *ismarried* specify an applicant's age and marital status, write an assignment statement that will result in the Boolean variable *iseligible* being assigned a value that reflects the specification in the advert.

Practical exercise 4.1

Write and run a program *inputcount* which requests a sequence of up to ten positive integers to be input one by one (i.e. one per line). As each integer is read in it is to be stored in the next available location in the array *store*; the first value input is to be stored in location 1. The input is to terminate when the integer input is negative or the array is full; the array is declared as

store: **array**[1..10] **of** integer;

The negative sentinel is not to be stored.

After the termination of the input the number of integers stored is to be written out and, if an attempt has been made to exceed the input limit of ten positive integers, this fact should also be noted in the output.

Note: there is no program template for this exercise.

Test your program with each of the following sets of input data

(i)   1 3 5 7 9 11 13 15 17 19 −8
(ii) 20 15 17 −6
(iii) −10
(iv) 2 4 6 8 10 1 3 5 7 9 15 18 20

Your program may vary slightly from the solution given. The test is whether or not it gives the correct output for the four sets of sample data.

4.4 Summary of section

This section was concerned with conditions. Simple conditions were discussed, and the use of the three Boolean operators **and, or** and **not** to produce compound conditions. If the condition holds it has the value *true*, otherwise it has the value *false*.

5 Multi-path selection

5.1 Card dealing revisited

We left the problem of dealing the cards in Section 2, at the program design stage, having prepared the detailed design shown in Figure 2.12. You will now need to refer to this design.

Notice that in the design to '*deal the hands*' many steps are taken up in the allocation of the card dealt to a particular hand. We used sixteen steps, from 4.2.4.1 to 4.2.4.16, to achieve this relatively simple operation. We may be tempted to estimate the number of steps required if we had more players! Our task was simply to select one of four hands; the choice being determined by the value of *player*. The difficulty was caused by the fact that the only control statement available, which would allow a selection of courses of action, was the **if** statement, allowing a choice between two alternatives. Hence, the strategy was implemented by *nesting* the **if** statements, that is arranging a succession of **if** statements, one inside another. The result, as you can see, is a lengthy and rather clumsy design.

What we need is a construct in which the desired course of action is determined immediately by the value of *player*. We shall, therefore, include the **case** construct in our design language. This enables a choice to be made between several courses of action, the selection being determined by the value to which a specified expression evaluates.

We require the selection to be made according to the value of the variable *player*. Using the **case** construct we can replace steps 4.2.4.1 to 4.2.4.16 of the design with the steps shown in Figure 5.1.

```
select case depending on player
    1: set appropriate element of hand1 to card
    2: set appropriate element of hand2 to card
    3: set appropriate element of hand3 to card
    4: set appropriate element of hand4 to card
    default: do nothing
selectend
```

Figure 5.1

Here, the default is taken if *player* does not have the value 1, 2, 3 or 4.

The **case** statement also allows for a number of values to trigger a particular course of action. So we can rewrite steps 4.2.2.1 to 4.2.2.6 of Figure 2.12 as shown in Figure 5.2.

```
select case depending on player
    1, 2, 3: set player to player + 1
    4: set player to 1
    default: do nothing
selectend
```

Figure 5.2

In this **case** construct, *player* is set to *player + 1* if *player* has the value 1, 2 or 3.

As another example consider the variable *digit* to be declared as

$$digit: 0..9;$$

We want to assign the value '*even*' to the string variable *balance* if the value of *digit* is 2, 4, 6 or 8, '*zero*' if the value of *digit* is 0, and '*odd*' if *digit* has the value 1, 3, 5, 7 or 9.

The following **case** construct can be used:

```
select case depending on digit
    2, 4, 6, 8: set balance to 'even'
    1, 3, 5, 7, 9: set balance to 'odd'
    0: set balance to 'zero'
    default: do nothing
selectend
```

Figure 5.3

5.2 The case statement in Pascal

The design in Figure 5.1 would be implemented in Pascal as shown in Figure 5.4.

```
case player of
    1: hand1[round] := card;
    2: hand2[round] := card;
    3: hand3[round] := card;
    4: hand4[round] := card
end
```

Figure 5.4

round is the number of the dealing round (see step 4.1 in Figure 2.12), an integer in the range 1..7. The default option has been ignored for the moment as there is no such option in Pascal. We shall consider this problem later.

The variable *player* is called the **case index** and the four constants 1, 2, 3 and 4 are known as **case labels**. In general the case index is an expression. Each option may be selected by more than one case label; the case labels form the **constant list**.

The general form of the **case** statement in Pascal is shown in Figure 5.5.

```
case expression of
    constant-list: statement;
    constant-list: statement;

    constant-list: statement
end
```

Figure 5.5

The values of the constants in the constant-lists must be of the same type as the expression. A statement can of course be a *compound statement*.

Exercise 5.1

Write a Pascal program to implement the designs shown in (a) Figure 5.2 and (b) Figure 5.3. Ignore the default option.

The **case** statement is executed as follows:

1 The case index is evaluated.

2 If the case index evaluates to one of the case labels, then the appropriate statement (or group of statements) is executed, else the case statement is bypassed and control passes to the first statement following the case statement.

3 After the execution of the selected statement (if any), the program continues with the next statement in sequence after the case statement.

Note the following points about the **case** statement (some of these will have already been mentioned; they are repeated here for completeness, so that this list may be used for reference).

(i)   It begins with the reserved word **case** and ends with **end**. There is no **begin**.

(ii) The values of the *constants* in the *constant list* (the *case labels*) are of the same type as the expression (*case*

index). No *constant* can appear more than once in a *constant list*.

(iii) Where a constant list contains more than one constant, the constants are separated by *commas* and the constants may be arranged in any order. Note that it is necessary to *list* all the constants in a constant list explicitly. For example, if the integers from 1 up to 15 are required they must all be explicitly listed:

1, 2, 3, 4, 5, 6, 7, 8, 9, 10, 11, 12, 13, 14, 15: statement;

abbreviations such as 1..15 are *not* permitted.

(iv) A constant list is separated from its statement(s) by a *colon*.

(v)   There must be at least one statement preceded by a constant list, i.e. there must be at least one specified path through the **case** statement.

(vi) In UCSD Pascal, when the case index does not evaluate to any of the case labels, the **case** statement is bypassed and the next statement in sequence is executed. We say that the **case** statement has 'fallen through'.

(vii) There is no default option in Pascal corresponding to the default situation in our design language. The default must be dealt with separately as we shall see.

(viii) After execution of the selected statements, the program continues with the next statement in sequence.

We have intentionally not specified the types that are allowed for the *case index* and the *case labels*. Of the types we have discussed so far; *integer*, *char*, subranges of *integer* and *char* and *Boolean* are acceptable types; types *real* and *string* are not allowed. We shall return to this topic in the next unit.

Exercise 5.2

Consider the following **case** statement:

```
case option of
    'A', 'a': astock:= astock − order;
    'B', 'b': bstock:= bstock − order;
    'C', 'c': begin
                writeln('this option is a discontinued line');
                satisfied:= false
              end;
end
```

option is a variable of type *char*, *astock*, *bstock* and *order* are of type *integer* and *satisfied* is a *Boolean* variable. If the values of *astock*, *bstock*, *order* and *satisfied* are 900, 650, 75 and true respectively, before the statement is executed, what are the values of these variables after the statement is executed, if *option* has the following values?

(i) *'b'*
(ii) *'c'*
(iii) *'N'*

Returning, now, to the *default* consideration, suppose that we wish to determine the number of days in a month, given the values of the *integer* variable *month* and the *Boolean* variable *isleapyear*. The following program segment will result in the appropriate value being assigned to the *integer* variable *monthlength*:

```
if (month > = 1) and (month < = 12)
then
    case month of
        1, 3, 5, 7, 8, 10, 12 : monthlength := 31;
        4, 6, 9, 11 : monthlength := 30;
        2 : if isleapyear
            then
                monthlength := 29
            else
                monthlength := 28
    end
else
    begin
        writeln('month invalid, monthlength set to zero');
        monthlength := 0
    end
```

Figure 5.6

Notice that in this example we tested the value of *month*, the case index, before the **case** statement was reached. This was necessary because *month* is an *integer* variable and the case labels only cover the range 1..12, so a default situation could arise. In circumstances such as this, where a default condition could arise, it is advisable to arrange the case statement so that it is incorporated in the **then** part of an **if** statement, and include the statements which comprise the default option in the **else** part.

In contrast to this, in Figure 5.3, the case index *digit* was a subrange type which was only allowed to take an *integer* value in the range 0..9. Since every value in this range appeared as a case label in one of the constant lists, a default condition was not possible, so it was not necessary to embed the **case** construct in an **if** statement. Note that in this type of situation the default condition is not possible, because any attempt to assign a value to the variable outside the specified subrange will result in an error being generated.

Exercise 5.3

In the program *choosedealer*, suppose it is required to write out details of the specific jack which is first out of the pack. Write a program segment which will use the value of *card*, which is assigned the value of the output of *random*, to write out

'the card is the jack of ———'

specifying the suit, if the card is jack and do nothing if the card identified is not a jack.

The examples and exercises used so far in this section have involved a single variable as the *case index*. However, as shown in Figure 5.5, the *case index* could be an expression. As an example consider the following situation:

The cost of sending packets by first-class mail is determined by their weight as shown in Figure 5.7.

Charge band	Weight in grams	Postage charge (pence)
1	up to 60	17
2	61–100	24
3	101–150	31
4	151–200	38
5	201–250	45
6	251–300	53
7	301–350	61 + 2p per 1000 km
8	351–400	69 + 2p per 1000 km
9	401–450	78 + 4p per 1000 km
10	451–500	87 + 4p per 1000 km

Figure 5.7

Note that there is a surcharge for letters weighing between 301 grams and 400 grams of 2 pence per complete 1000 kilometres; for weights between 401 grams and 500 grams the surcharge is 4 pence per complete 1000 kilometres. Items weighing more than 500 grams are not allowed.

Suppose it is required to write a program to take, as input, the weight of the item rounded up to the nearest gram and to write out the postage charge.

The top-level design for the program would be as shown in Figure 5.8.

```
1  input a valid weight in grams
2  input the distance in kilometres
3  determine the postage charge
4  write out the postage charge
```

Figure 5.8

Step 1 can be refined to a loop that checks that only weights not greater than 500 grams are input (Figure 5.9).

```
1.1  loop
1.2     read in a value for weight
1.3  until (weight < = 500) and (weight > 0)
1.4  loopend
```

Figure 5.9

The third step involves an examination of the charges table. Notice that there are ten weight bands, the last eight of which are of size 50 grams. The first two weight bands are of different sizes. We can construct a mathematical formula to establish the charge band for items with a weight in the range 101..500, but the first two bands must be treated separately.

To construct the formula we require the integer operator **div**. This operator requires *two* integer operands, the second of which cannot be zero. The operator yields the *integer part* of the result obtained by dividing the first operand by the second.

So 40 **div** 7 gives the result 5

18 **div** 6 gives the result 3

19 **div** 6 gives the result 3

SAQ 5.1

Evaluate the following expressions

```
Evaluate the following expressions
(i)        24 div 5
(ii)        6 div 8
(iii)      35 div 8 + 2
(iv)       34 div 6 = 6
```

div is evaluated before +

Solution 5.1

```
(i)      4
(ii)     0
(iii)    6
(iv)     false
```
35 div 8 gives the result 4

Our formula, then, is obtained as follows: If we number the weight charge bands 1 to 10 the formula

(*weight* + 49) **div** 50

gives the appropriate charge band for an item with a weight in the range 101..500 (grams).

SAQ 5.2

Using the formula

(*weight* + 49) **div** 50

determine the number of the charge band for each of the following values of the variable *weight*

(i) 140   (ii) 300   (iii) 401   (iv) 409

Solution 5.2

(i) 3   (ii) 6   (iii) 9   (iv) 9

A detailed design for the program might be as shown in Figure 5.10.

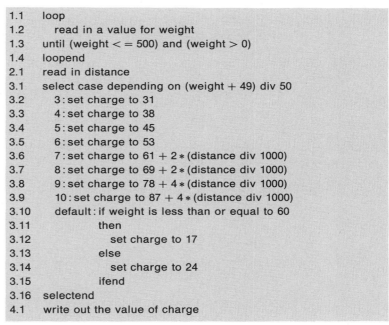

```
1.1   loop
1.2      read in a value for weight
1.3   until (weight < = 500) and (weight > 0)
1.4   loopend
2.1   read in distance
3.1   select case depending on (weight + 49) div 50
3.2       3 : set charge to 31
3.3       4 : set charge to 38
3.4       5 : set charge to 45
3.5       6 : set charge to 53
3.6       7 : set charge to 61 + 2 * (distance div 1000)
3.7       8 : set charge to 69 + 2 * (distance div 1000)
3.8       9 : set charge to 78 + 4 * (distance div 1000)
3.9      10 : set charge to 87 + 4 * (distance div 1000)
3.10     default : if weight is less than or equal to 60
3.11            then
3.12               set charge to 17
3.13            else
3.14               set charge to 24
3.15           ifend
3.16  selectend
4.1   write out the value of charge
```

Figure 5.10

The data table for this program is shown in Figure 5.11 and the full program listing is shown in Figure 5.12.

Identifier	Description	Type
weight	weight of the item in grams	integer variable
distance	distance letter will travel in kilometres	integer variable
charge	postage charge in pence (p)	integer variable

Figure 5.11

```
program charges;
var
    weight, charge, distance:integer;
begin
    writeln('This program calculates the first class postage charges');
    writeln('for items weighing NOT MORE THAN 500 grams');
    write('What is the weight of your item rounded upto the ');
    write('nearest gram? ');
    repeat
        readln(weight)
    until (weight <= 500) and (weight > 0);
        writeln('Type the distance the packet is to travel in km');
        readln(distance);
    if weight > 100
    then
        case (weight + 49) div 50 of
            3: charge:= 31;
            4: charge:= 38;
            5: charge:= 45;
            6: charge:= 53;
            7: charge:= 61 + 2 * (distance div 1000);
            8: charge:= 69 + 2 * (distance div 1000);
            9: charge:= 78 + 4 * (distance div 1000);
           10: charge:= 87 + 4 * (distance div 1000);
        end
    else
        if weight <= 60
        then
            charge:= 17
        else
            charge:= 24;
    writeln('First class postage charge is ', charge, 'p')
end.
```

Figure 5.12

Practical exercise 5.1 _____

Write a program called *findsuit* which will accept, as input, an integer in the range 1..52 and, assuming that this integer represents a playing card, write out the suit of the card represented. Take, as a convention, the representation outlined in Section 2.1 of this unit: integers 1 to 13 represent clubs, 14 to 26 represent diamonds, etc.

Your program should use a **case** statement and the operator **div**. Structure the program so that the user is given the option of repeating the cycle as many times as is required.

Run your program and test it using the following sequence of input values:

4, 25, 84, 33, 48

A program that satisfies the requirements of the exercise is given at the end of the unit; your program may be slightly different.

There is no program template for this exercise.

When you run your program you should obtain the results shown in Figure 5.13.

input	output
4	The suit is clubs
25	The suit is diamonds
84	⟵ this input is ignored
33	The suit is hearts
48	The suit is spades

Figure 5.13

You should also test to ensure that your program only accepts 'y' or 'n' as the answer to the continue question.

Points to check for in your program:

1 Only integers in the range 1..52 accepted as input for *card*. (The program should repeatedly ask for input, specifying range, until acceptable input is obtained)

2 The **case** statement gives correct options. (Notice that having ensured that the input is in the correct range we do not require a default option)

3 When the question 'do you want to repeat?' is asked, only the valid responses 'y' or 'n' are accepted. (The question should repeatedly appear specifying the acceptable responses until user complies)

5.3 Implementing the program *dealhands* in Pascal

In the previous section we discussed points relating to the program *dealhands* and in Figure 5.4 and Exercise 5.1 we implemented parts of the design. In this section we shall develop the second part of the design in Figure 2.12 and build the program to deal the hands.

In Exercise 5.1 we implemented steps 4.2.2.1 to 4.2.2.6 of Figure 2.12. In Figure 5.4 we dealt with steps 4.2.4.1 to 4.2.4.16. Now we only need to implement steps 4.2.3.1 to 4.2.3.4 and step 4.4. You may recall that the section of the design between 4.2.3.1 and 4.2.3.4 is repeatedly generating integers in the range 1..52 until an integer is obtained that identifies a card which is still in the pack. We have already solved this problem for the program *choosedealer*.

Exercise 5.4

Write the program segment to implement steps 4.2.3.1 to 4.2.3.4 of the design in Figure 2.12 using a *postconditioned* loop.

Exercise 5.5

Use the program segments that have been developed to implement steps 4.2.1.1 to 4.2.5 of the design.

In the **case** statements that appear, a default situation is not needed since it would be preferable to refuse to accept an input value for *player* that is invalid.

In the last exercise we suggested that it is better, to refuse to accept invalid values as input; such values cause a proliferation of **if** statements in the program. We have illustrated this technique in the context of the program *charges* (Figure 5.12) and in Practical exercise 5.1.

Figure 2.12 is the complete design to 'choose a dealer' and 'deal the hands'. At the end of the first part of the design to 'choose a dealer' the variable *player* contains the identity of the dealer and this is used in the second part of the design. We have already implemented the first part but to implement the second part, 'deal the hands', we must know the identity of the dealer. As we are implementing them separately, the identity of the dealer must be input into the program. This can be implemented as a 'repeat until' loop as shown in Figure 5.14.

```
repeat
    writeln('Input the identity of the dealer');
    writeln('(an integer in the range 1..4)');
    readln(dealer)
until (dealer >= 1) and (dealer <= 4);
player := dealer
```

Figure 5.14

All that remains to be refined is step 4.4 of Figure 2.12, which writes out the contents of each hand. We suggest you use a **for** loop to do this for each of the hands.

Practical exercise 5.2

Complete the program *dealhands* and run your program. Test it by inputting values which are out of range before you supply a valid integer.

You may wish to refer to the listing of *choosedealer* in Figure 2.14 since, like *choosedealer*, the *dealhands* program requires the unit *udealer*. You will need to have copies of the following files onto your user disk:

B2:UDEALER.CODE
B2:DDEALER.TEXT

A complete program listing for this exercise appears at the end of this unit.

(Note that you may have adopted a different strategy for the details of the output of the hands from ours.)

5.4 Summary of section

In this section of the unit we used aspects of the implementation of the card dealing problem design to introduce the **case** statement in Pascal. This construct can be used when a choice has to be made between several courses of action depending upon the value of an expression.

After an analysis of the various aspects of the use of the **case** statement, the program *dealhands* was implemented in Pascal. In this section we also introduced the operator **div**, which gives the integer part of the result obtained by dividing one operand by another.

Summary of unit

In this unit we have completed our introduction to the control structures that you will meet in this course. Without these structures a program would be executed in strict sequential statement order, which would severely limit the useful employment of computers. The ability to achieve selective and repetitive execution of statements is essential for any practical use of the computer.

The control structures you have used are

> if...then...else
> the case statement
> the while statement
> the repeat statement
> the for statement

The last three of these structures enable us to achieve repetition of one or more statements. We have also classified the control structures according to the following two criteria:

(i) When the condition is evaluated in relation to the statements to be repeated.

(ii) The nature of the control of the repetition.

The former criterion gives rise to the terms *preconditioned* and *postconditioned*; the while statement is in the *preconditioned* category and the repeat statement is classified as *postconditioned*.

The second of the two criteria distinguishes loops which are dynamically controlled from those in which the number of repetitions is determined before the loop is executed. In this case, the repeat and while statements are distinguished from the for statement; the latter is classified as a loop with a predetermined number of repetitions at execution time.

The if...then...else and case constructs are used when a choice needs to be made between different courses of action. The if statement enables us to select *one* of *two* alternative paths, the direction taken depends on the value taken by a condition or Boolean expression. Where a *number* of alternative courses of action are possible the case statement is used.

Some of the concepts discussed in this unit will receive further attention in the next unit. We shall also return to the card playing problem.

Solutions to exercises

Solution 2.1

Identifier	Description	Type
player	identity of player receiving next card	integer variable
dealer	identity of dealer	integer variable
card	variable to which output of random number generator is assigned	integer variable
k	loop control variable for step 1.1	integer variable
pack	array representing a pack of cards which indicates cards left in the pack and those which have been dealt	array [1..52] of Boolean variable

Solution 2.2

```
type cardarray = array[1..52] of Boolean;
var
    player, card, k: integer;
    pack: cardarray;
    dealer: integer;
```

Solution 2.3

```
for k := 1 to 52 do
    pack[k] := true
```

Solution 3.1

```
2.3.7    loop
2.3.8        generate an integer, card, using random
2.3.9    until pack[card] is true
2.3.10   loopend
```

These four steps replace the four steps 2.3.7 to 2.3.10.

Solution 3.2

(i)

```
1  read in an integer
2  loop while integer is
       non-negative
3      write out a row of
           asterisks of appropriate
           length
4      read in an integer
5  loopend
```

(ii)

```
1  read in an integer
2  loop
3      write out a row of
           asterisks of appropriate
           length
4      read in an integer
5  until integer is negative
6  loopend
```

Solution 3.3

(i) (a) Move elements in locations 40 down to 17 one location so that they occupy locations 41 to 18

(b) Insert *newe1* into location 17

(c) Increment the variable *stockitems*

(ii)

```
for index := 40 downto 17 do
    parts[index + 1] := parts[index];
parts[17] := newe1;
stockitems := stockitems + 1
```

Note that it is more natural to use a **for downto** loop to implement (a) since we must move from the higher index down to the lower. The element in location 40 must be moved to location 41 *before* the element in location 39 is moved in to location 40.

Solution 4.1

(i) *number* has an integer value greater than 4 and *total* has an integer value greater than or equal to 100. Both of these conditions must be satisfied.

(ii) The value of *colour* must be either 'r' or 'w' (notice that in this case both conditions can't be true.)

(iii) At least one of the conditions *success* is false, *number* has a value less than *maxval*, is true.

(iv) Either *number* has a value between 0 and 10 or *success* is true, or both conditions may be true. (Again note the brackets here to ensure that > and < are evaluated first, then **and**, then **or**.)

(v) Both conditions **not** (*number* < 20) **and** (*number* > 10) must be true. For the former to be true the value of *number* must be greater than or equal to 20. Thus, the latter condition is automatically satisfied and could be omitted.

(vi) This condition is not satisfied for any value of *number* since *number* cannot be both greater than or equal to 20 and less than 10.

Solution 4.2

(i) $(month >= 1)$ **and** $(month <= 12)$
(Note there are variations on this theme which are equally acceptable involving the testing of *month* for values greater than zero and less than 13. Of course the order of the component conditions could be reversed.)

(ii) $(answer = 'y')$ **or** $(answer = 'yes')$

(iii) **not** *stop* **and** $(index > start)$

(iv) $(ordertotal > 12)$ **or not** $((city = location)$ **or** $(city = depot))$. Alternative answers to this question include $(ordertool > 12)$ **or** $((city <> location)$ **and** $(city <> depot))$, $(ordertotal > 12)$ **or** $(($**not** $(city = location)$ **and not** $(city = depot))$. In addition to these, $(ordertotal > 12)$ may be replaced by $(ordertotal >= 13)$.

Solution 4.3

(i)

```
positive := false;
zero := false;
negative := false;
if number > 0 then
   positive := true
else
   if number = 0 then
      zero := true
   else
      negative := true
```

Note that the three Boolean variables are all initialized to *false*. The processing assigns the value *true* to the appropriate one.

(ii)

```
if (month = 1) and ((day >= 1)
                and (day <= 31))
then
   datevalid := true
else
   datevalid := false
```

A neater solution to this problem is

```
datevalid := (month = 1) and (day >= 1)
                         and (day <= 31)
```

datevalid as set is *true* if the three conditions on the right-hand side are all *true*.

Solution 4.4

(i)

```
ismybirthday := (day = 16) and (month = 11)
```

(ii)

```
iseligible := not ismarried and (age >= 25)
                           and (age <= 35)
```

Note: Brackets are not required around **not** *ismarried* because of precedence rules but it is not incorrect to include them.

Solution 5.1

(a)

```
case player of
   1, 2, 3: player := player + 1;
   4: player := 1
end
```

(b)

```
case digit of
   2, 4, 6, 8: balance := 'even';
   1, 3, 5, 7, 9: balance := 'odd';
   0: balance := 'zero'
end
```

Solution 5.2

(i) $astock = 900$ $bstock = 575$, $order = 75$, $satisfied = true$
The value of *bstock* is changed, the values of the other variables remain unchanged.

(ii) $astock = 900$ $bstock = 650$, $order = 75$ and $satisfied = false$
This time the third option is taken and only *satisfied* is assigned a new value.

(iii) In this instance the value of the *case index* does not match any of the *case labels* and the statement 'falls through' leaving all four variables unchanged.

Solution 5.3

```
if (card = 11) or (card = 24) or (card = 37) or (card = 50)
then
   case card of
      11: writeln('The card is the jack of clubs');
      24: writeln('The card is the jack of diamonds');
      37: writeln('The card is the jack of hearts');
      50: writeln('The card is the jack of spades')
   end
```

Notice that the **case** statement from the reserved word **case** to the reserved word **end** is a single statement so it does not require bracketing by **begin** and **end**.

Solution 5.4

```
repeat
   card := random
until pack[card]
```

Note that **until** *pack[card]* is equivalent to **until** *pack[card]* = *true* since *pack* is an array of *Boolean*.

Solution 5.5 _____

```
for repetition := 1 to 4 do
   begin
      case player of
         1, 2, 3 : player := player + 1;
         4 : player := 1
      end;
      repeat
         card := random
      until pack[card];
      case player of
         1 : hand1[round] := card;
         2 : hand2[round] := card;
         3 : hand3[round] := card;
         4 : hand4[round] := card
      end
   end
```

Solutions to practical exercises

Solution to Practical exercise 2.1 _____

For part (iii) you might have inserted the statement

```
writeln('card = ', card)
```

immediately after each *card := random* statement and a statement

```
writeln('card dealt is identified by the integer', card)
```

immediately after each *pack[card] := false* statement.

Solution to Practical exercise 3.1 _____

```
program postlinear;
{initializes and linearly searches the array
          ladder}
{uses a Pascal unit for initializing the array}
uses {$u ulinear1.code} ulinear1;
const
  size = 10;
type
  listtype = array [0..size] of string;
var
  index : integer;
  ladder : listtype;
  search_item : string;
begin
  initialize(ladder);
  write('Input name to be searched for ');
  readln(search_item);
  ladder[0] := search_item;
  index := size + 1;
  repeat
    index := index − 1
  until ladder[index] = search_item;
  if index = 0
  then
    writeln('Name is not in ladder')
  else
    writeln('Name found at index ', index)
end.
```

Solution to Practical exercise 4.1 _____

```
program inputcount;
var
  store : array [1..10] of integer;
  value : integer;
  index : integer;
```

```
begin
  writeln('Input up to 10 positive integers, one by one');
  write('The sequence is to be terminated by ');
  writeln('a negative integer');
  index := 0;
  write('What is your first integer? ');
  readln(value);
  while (value > 0) and (index < 10) do
    begin
      index := index + 1;
      store[index] := value;
      write('Next integer? ');
      readln(value)
    end;
  if value > 0
  then
    begin
      write('You have input more positive integers ');
      writeln('than the program allows');
      write('Consequently, 10 have been stored and ');
      writeln('the 11th has been ignored');
    end
  else
    writeln(index, 'positive integers have been stored');
end.
```

Solution to Practical exercise 5.1 _____

```
program findsuit;
var
  answer : char;
  card : integer;
begin
  writeln('This program accepts an integer in the range 1..52');
  writeln(' as input and writes out the suit of the card');
  writeln(' represented by this integer');
  answer := 'y';
  while answer = 'y' do
    begin
      repeat
        write('Input an integer in the range 1..52 ');
        readln(card)
      until (card > 0) and (card < 53);
      case (card + 12) div 13 of
        1 : writeln('The suit is clubs');
        2 : writeln('The suit is diamonds');
        3 : writeln('The suit is hearts');
        4 : writeln('The suit is spades')
      end;
      repeat
        write('Do you want to input another integer? (y/n) ');
        readln(answer)
      until (answer = 'y') or (answer = 'n')
    end;
  writeln('Program finished')
end.
```

Solution to Practical exercise 5.2 _____

```
program dealhands;
uses {$u udealer.code} udealer;
type
    hand = array [1..7] of integer;
var
    player, dealer: integer;
    round, repetition: integer;
    card, p, k: integer;
    pack: array [1..52] of Boolean;
    hand1, hand2, hand3, hand4: hand;
begin
    {input the identity of the dealer}
    repeat
        write('Input the identity of the dealer');
        write('(an integer in the range 1..4)');
        readln(dealer)
    until (dealer >= 1) and (dealer <= 4);
    player := dealer;
    {prepare the pack for dealing}
    for k := 1 to 52 do
        pack[k] := true;
    {start the deal: seven rounds, i.e. seven cards to each player}
    for round := 1 to 7 do
        begin
            for repetition := 1 to 4 do
                begin
                    {select next player}
                    case player of
                        1, 2, 3: player := player + 1;
                        4: player := 1
                    end;
                    {deal a card}
                    repeat
                        card := random
                    until pack[card];
                    pack[card] := false;
                    {insert card in players hand}
                    case player of
                        1: hand1[round] := card;
                        2: hand2[round] := card;
                        3: hand3[round] := card;
                        4: hand4[round] := card
                    end
                end
            {each player has now received one card in this round}
            {move on to next round}
        end;
    {write out the contents of each hand}
    writeln;
    write('The details of the hands dealt to the four players');
    writeln('are as follows:');
    writeln;
    writeln('player number 1:');
    for p := 1 to 7 do
        write(' ', hand1[p]);
    writeln;
    writeln('player number 2:');
    for p := 1 to 7 do
        write(' ', hand2[p]);
    writeln;
    writeln('player number 3:');
    for p := 1 to 7 do
        write(' ', hand3[p]);
    writeln;
    writeln('player number 4:');
    for p := 1 to 7 do
        write(' ', hand4[p]);
    writeln
end.
```

Unit 4 More on Types

Prepared by the Course Team

Contents

Study guide

This unit introduces you to a number of new data types and illustrates their uses in a variety of situations.

The introduction is very short and will take only a minute or two to read through.

Section 2 introduces the enumeration type. Hopefully you will find that this is a straightforward section, but do not rush through it, for much of this unit subsequently depends on the ideas introduced here. Many of these ideas also crop up frequently in the remainder of the course. The section ends with a practical activity.

Section 3 illustrates the use of enumeration types as control variables with **for** loops. The most important material is contained in the first subsection. The remaining text can be read fairly briskly. Subsection 3.3 previews the Pascal functions *succ* and *pred* which will reappear in *Block III*.

Section 4 returns to arrays and their uses. The only novelty is the appearance of enumeration type and character variables for fulfilling the role of the array index. If you have understood the earlier work on arrays then this section should prove to be routine; if not, it should help you to master this topic. The section contains one substantial practical exercise.

Your pacing through the unit should leave you plenty of time for Sections 5 and 6 which contain a new topic—two-dimensional arrays and their applications. You will encounter two-dimensional arrays in the remainder of the course, so it is essential that you try to master the ideas here and now.

Section 5 is reasonably short, but there is a good deal of practice in navigating around arrays using a pair of array indexes. A good appreciation of this material is crucial, so do not cut corners when you study it.

In Section 6 we develop a relatively complex problem solution (involving a two-dimensional array) right through to a working program.

Study plan

Section		Media required	Time
1	Introduction	Text	
2	Enumeration types	Text, HCF	1 evening
3	Enumeration types and **for** loops	Text, HCF	1 evening
4	Other uses for ordinal data types	Text, HCF	1 evening
5	Multi-dimensional arrays	Text	1 evening
6	A practical example	Text, HCF	1 evening
	Summary	Text	

1 *Introduction*

In the early stages of learning programming there is a tendency to concentrate attention on the design of algorithms, and on the subsequent coding of that design into Pascal, or some other programming language. However, as we begin to encounter more complex programs, the importance of careful organization of the data gains prominence. The right selection of data representation can simplify the design of algorithms and greatly increase the efficiency of the final program. In previous units of this block we have introduced the *array structure*, and through numerous examples we are beginning to appreciate its usefulness and potential. In this unit we are going to extend our range of data types, by introducing and exploring the uses of more data structures.

Sections 2, 3 and 4 hinge around one notion. Quite often in programming we find a need for variables which are confined to a restricted range of values. For example, we may have an *integer* variable which, through interpretation of its role in a particular problem, might only be allowed to take values from 0 to 9 inclusive. Alternatively, in a problem which involves five sets of data, one for each weekday, it might be convenient to employ a variable which can take just five values; monday, tuesday, wednesday, thursday and friday. Whenever we can list (i.e. enumerate) all the values that a variable is to be permitted to take, Pascal allows us to define an appropriate type, which is generically called an *enumeration type*. We shall investigate the use and limitations of the *enumeration type*. One interesting feature on which we shall capitalize is that an enumeration type is *ordered*; the order is implied by the order in which the values of the type are listed in the *type definition*.

One type where all permitted values can be *listed* is of particular importance. When the values form a *consecutive* set of integers, or of characters, or of values of an enumeration type, Pascal permits definition of a *subrange type*. For example, the integers from 0 to 9 inclusive are the possible values in the *subrange type* 0..9 *of integer*. We shall see that there are a variety of benefits to be gained through use of subrange types, particularly in their natural use for *indexing* arrays.

In Sections 5 and 6 we shall turn to extensions of the array concept. We shall concentrate mainly on two-dimensional arrays and their uses. Any table of data, where the entries are all of the same *base type*, is naturally represented by a *two-dimensional array*. As such phenomena occur very frequently in problems, the two-dimensional array is an important tool in the programmer's armoury.

Section 5 provides practice in the use of the two indexes, needed to locate elements of a two-dimensional array, for storing and retrieving appropriate data. In Section 6 we consolidate many of the ideas introduced in this unit, in the context of solving a complex problem involving the use of a two-dimensional array.

2 *Enumeration types*

2.1 Ordinal and structured data types

So far in the course we have become familiar with four simple data types; *integer*, *real*, *char* and *Boolean*. We have also met two further types, *string* and *array*. These latter types are called *structured data types* because they are built up from the simple types; an *array* is constructed from elements of its *base type* whilst a *string* is built out of elements of *type char*.

The simple data types themselves fall into two categories:

(i) *real*: consisting of the type *real*
(ii) *ordinal*: consisting of *integer*, *char* and *Boolean*.

The two categories *real* and *ordinal* are distinguished by the fact that the *ordinals* can be *enumerated*, that is, can be *listed in order*. To be a little more precise, if we are given any two members of the same ordinal type, then all members of that type lying between the two given ones can be listed in order. The *reals do not* have this property because, although they are ordered, we cannot list *all* the *real* numbers lying between 1 and 2, for example.

Thus, we can picture data types as shown in Figure 2.1.

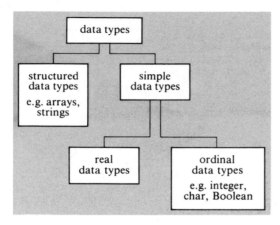

Figure 2.1

In this unit we shall capitalize on the ability to enumerate elements of an *ordinal type*. We shall see numerous problems in which *ordinal data* occurs naturally, but not necessarily in one of the forms *integer*, *char*, or *Boolean*. Pascal provides a facility to enable us to define our own *ordinal types*. These *user-defined ordinal types* go by a variety of names in textbooks; *scalar types*, *enumerated types* or *enumeration types*. We shall use the name *enumeration type* in this course.

2.2 Examples of enumeration types

In designing solutions to problems, one important aspect which this block should be impressing upon you, and subsequent work certainly will, is the importance of selecting the correct data structures to represent the data in the problem. In a problem concerning a column of figures we would make use of an appropriate *numerical array*; where a table is involved we use *parallel arrays* (although we shall introduce a more natural data structure using *records* in *Block IV*). Selection of data structures is a key step in the design of a solution. Quite often a programmer will find that none of the types available to him provide suitable values for description of the data that he wishes to incorporate into his program. For example, in a program to collate and analyse monthly unemployment figures over a year, we could envisage using a variable *month* which could take any of twelve values; January, February, March, ... or December. A program which concerns the colours of the spectrum might profitably use a variable which can take any of seven values red, orange, yellow, green, blue, indigo and violet. Pascal allows the programmer to define his own data types whenever he can list all the possible values.

Enumeration type definitions appear in the declarations part of the program. Each definition is of the form

type *identifier* = (*list of values*);

with the chosen name for the **type** on the left and a listing of all the values that a variable of the **type** will be allowed to take on the right enclosed in round brackets. Each of the values takes the form of an identifier; that is, a *letter* followed (optionally) by a string of letters and digits. For example,

spectrum = (red, orange, yellow, green, blue, indigo, violet);

suit = (clubs, diamonds, hearts, spades);

subject = (art, english, french, german, history, geography, mathematics, physics, chemistry, biology);

tenprimes = (p2, p3, p5, p7, p11, p13, p17, p19, p23, p29);

Note that, in the *enumerated list* of values, the *same* value *cannot* be included more than once.

Variables of these new types are defined in the **var** declarations, just like other variables, as shown in Figure 2.2.

var
    trumps: suit;
    foreground: spectrum;
    nextlesson, examination: subject;
    divisor: tenprimes;

Figure 2.2

SAQ 2.1

Write suitable enumeration type definitions to represent the following data.

(i)   The days of the week.
(ii) The vowels of the alphabet (in lower case).
(iii) The states of traffic lights.
(iv) The pieces on a chess board.

Solution

(i)   day = (sun, mon, tues, wed, thur, fri, sat);
(ii) vowel = (a, e, i, o, u);
(iii) state = (green, amber, red, redamber);
(iv) piece = (WQ, WK, WB, WR, WN, WP, BQ, BK, BB, BR, BN, BP);

We have used accepted abbreviations WR for White Rook, BQ for Black Queen, etc.

Having declared a variable of some enumeration type it can be used in programs just like any other variable. It can be assigned values, updated and used in **case** statements and expressions. Figure 2.3 contains a little program which simulates the traffic-light sequence, using the enumeration type *state* declared in SAQ 2.1. Read through the program and see if you can sort out exactly what it is doing before reading the commentary which follows.

```
program traffic_lights;
type state = (green, amber, red, redamber);
var ch: char;
    light: state;
begin
  light:= redamber;
  ch:= ' ';
  while ch = ' ' do
  begin
    case light of
      green    : begin
                   light:= amber;
                   writeln('The lights are at amber')
                 end;
      amber    : begin
                   light:= red;
                   writeln('The lights are at red')
                 end;
      red      : begin
                   light:= redamber;
                   writeln('The lights are at red and amber')
                 end;
      redamber: begin
                   light:= green;
                   writeln('The lights are at green')
                 end
    end; {of case}
    writeln('Type space to continue sequence or any other key to stop it');
    read(ch)
  end {of while loop}
end.
```

Figure 2.3

In the program in Figure 2.3 we have defined a **type** *state* and declared a variable *light* of **type** *state*. So the variable *light* can take any one of the four listed values, corresponding to the four colour states of a traffic light. The program declares a second variable, *ch* of **type** *char*. The first two lines of the program body initialize the variables, *light* being assigned the value *redamber*. Moving on a few lines, the major part of the program is a single **case** statement, which should be self-explanatory; the value of *light* is updated to the next in the traffic light sequence starting at red and amber and the appropriate information written out. The **case** statement is contained within a **while** loop controlled by the character *ch* which is updated by the user from the keyboard. While the user selects the space character the loop continues.

Notice also that the variable used as the case selector is of **type** *state*. We mentioned in *Unit 3* that the only variables allowed as case selector were *integer*, *char* or *Boolean*. We can now add the new *user-defined ordinal type* to this former list of *ordinal types*; the case selector can be any *ordinal type*.

SAQ 2.2 _____

(i) The loop in the traffic lights program is executed at least once. Why is this?
(ii) Trace the output of the program if the user selects the space character twice and then a non-space character.

Solution 2.2

(i) The character *ch* controlling the loop is initialized to the space character and the loop is executed once before the user has an opportunity to change this value in the *read(ch)* statement.
(ii) The output would be:

The lights are at green.
Type space to continue sequence, or any other key to stop it.
The lights are at amber.
Type space to continue sequence, or any other key to stop it.
The lights are at red.
Type space to continue sequence, or any other key to stop it.

In the program in Figure 2.3, it is important to realize that, no matter how much they may resemble *strings*, *green*, *amber*, *red* and *redamber* are *not string* values. They are values of **type** *state*. *String* values *cannot* be assigned to variables of **type** *state*, nor can they be compared with values of **type** *state*. For example, each of the statements:

```
light: = 'green';
```

and

```
if light = 'green'
then ...
```

would result in syntactic errors because of a mismatch of types; *'green'* is a *string constant* whilst *light* is *not a string variable*. Attempting to assign *string* values to a variable of *enumeration type* is a common programming error. Also, variables of an *enumeration type cannot* be 'read in', or

'written out'. This will be considered further in the next section.

Even though the listed values of an enumeration type are not string values, they are nevertheless sequences of characters. So did we really need the *enumeration type state* in the traffic-lights program? Could we not have simply declared the variable *light* to be of **type** *string* and written essentially the same program but amended it by enclosing every occurrence of *green*, *amber*, *red* and *redamber* in apostrophes to make them *string* values? Well, no we cannot, because Pascal does not permit the **type** *string* as case selector.

So, we have seen one use of the enumeration type. It can improve the readability and comprehension of programs. There is, however, a second and more important benefit from using the enumeration type. The type definition gives us tighter control over the values of variables. For instance, when we declare a variable to be of **type** *string* then we are permitting it to take any of infinitely many *string* values. Suppose, however, that in reality, it can only take (say) four values. Now, in a complex program, where the value of this variable is changing frequently, we would need to build in some check against it acquiring extraneous, unmeaningful values. On the other hand, defining it to be an enumeration type and listing all its possible values has a built-in safeguard against this. Any attempt to assign a value that is not one of its listed values to such a variable would produce a syntactic error which the compiler would recognize and report. We shall see good examples of this later when we use type definitions to confine numerical data to appropriate ranges of values.

2.3 Using enumeration types in control statements

Consider the design extract in Figure 2.4.

```
select case depending on choice
    continue : repeat the application
    stop     : exit the program
    error    : report error in input data
    default  : do nothing
selectend
```

Figure 2.4

We could imagine this extract as being part of a top-level solution to a problem in which an application is repeated under the control of the user. For example, the user may be inputting data and for each input of valid data the application is repeated until a sentinel value indicates the end of input.

Notice how the use of the words *continue*, *stop* and *error* make the structure and purpose of the *case* selection obvious, although we still lack details of the actions to be taken for each of the selections. To preserve this structure, when we implement the design in Pascal, we shall need to define an enumeration type as shown in Figure 2.5.

```
...
type selection = (continue, stop, error);
var  choice : selection;
......
  case choice of
      continue : begin
                    {code for this choice}
                 end;
      stop     : begin
                    {code for this choice}
                 end;
      error    : begin
                    {code for this choice}
                 end
  end; {of case}
```

Figure 2.5

Again note how the use of the enumeration type has enabled the program to reflect closely the designer's intentions.

Exercise 2.1

Write down the suitable type definitions and variable declarations, and write code similar in detail to that of Figure 2.5 to reflect the design extract in Figure 2.6.

```
select case depending on transaction
   cash        : process cash transaction
   cheque      : process cheque transaction
   credit      : process credit transaction
   credit-card : process credit-card transaction
selectend
```

Figure 2.6

We shall now write a complete program along these lines, using an enumeration type variable to control the program flow. The purpose of the program is to accumulate scores input by the user and give, on request, the *average* of the scores input so far. The input from the user will determine whether more numbers are to follow, or the average is to be computed, or the session is to be terminated and the final average computed. We shall assume that the scores are positive integers in the range 1 to some maximum which we shall call *maxscore*. Any input exceeding *maxscore* is in error. A design is shown in Figure 2.7.

```
1   initialize variables
2   loop
3       read in score
4       determine action
5       select case depending on action
6           continue : process score
7           error    : write out error message
8           analyse  : write out analysis of scores so far
9           stop     : write out final analysis
10      selectend
11  until action = stop
12  loopend
```

Figure 2.7

To determine the average of a collection of numbers we shall need to keep track of the accumulated sum of the valid integers input, and how many there are of them. For these purposes we shall use the variables *sum* and *count*, respectively. Our data table is shown in Figure 2.8.

Identifier	Description	Type
score	scores to be averaged, entered from the keyboard	integer variable
action	values are continue, error, analyse and stop	enumeration type variable
sum	the total of the valid scores entered	integer variable
count	the number of valid scores entered	integer variable
average	sum divided by (non-zero) count	real variable
maxscore	the maximum permitted score	integer constant

Figure 2.8

Our description of the variable *score* is far from complete, because the input values of *score* are going to have to be used for other purposes. We need a sentinel value to indicate when all input is complete (so that *action* is set to *stop*), and also a value to indicate a request for the *average* so far to be determined and written out. We shall make the following design decisions. An input of 0 will be used to request the *average* so far, and an input of any negative number will indicate termination of input. So we can draw up a table for converting values of *score* to the determined value of *action* as shown in Figure 2.9.

score	action
negative	stop
0	analyse
1 to *maxscore*	continue
exceeding *maxscore*	error

Figure 2.9

This is precisely the information needed to refine step 4.

Exercise 2.2 _____
Refine step 4.

The remaining steps which require further refinement, namely 1, 3, 6, 7, 8 and 9, are all straightforward. If you feel you need further practice try the refinements now without reading on. Our final design is shown in Figure 2.10.

In our development of this program we have not yet given a type identifier for the enumeration type of which *action* is a variable.

In fact, we do not have to select a name because the enumeration type can be defined implicitly in a **var** description. For example;

var *action*: *(continue, error, analyse, stop);*

declares *action* to be a variable of an *unnamed* enumeration type which takes the four listed values. In this course we shall use both methods of making type definitions. More often than not, for clarity, we shall include a type identifier and we advocate that you do the same, but as the course progresses we shall make increasing use of the implicit definition in certain settings.

To round off this section we ask you to implement the design in Figure 2.10 as a practical exercise.

```
1.1    set sum to 0
1.2    set count to 0
2      loop
3.1        prompt for input
3.2        read in score
4.1        set action to continue
4.2        if score < 1
4.3        then
4.4            if score = 0
4.5            then
4.6                set action to analyse
4.7            else
4.8                set action to stop
4.9            ifend
4.10       else
4.11           if score > maxscore
4.12           then
4.13               set action to error
4.14           else
4.15               do nothing
4.16           ifend
4.17       ifend
5          select case depending on action
6.1            continue : increment count
6.2                       set sum to sum + score
7              error    : write out that score exceeds maxscore
8.1            analyse  : if count > 0
8.2                       then
8.3                           set average to sum/count
8.4                           write out average
8.5                       else
8.6                           write out error message
8.7                       ifend
9.1            stop     : if count > 0
9.2                       then
9.3                           set average to sum/count
9.4                           write out average
9.5                       else
9.6                           write out error message
9.7                       ifend
10         selectend
11     until action = stop
12     loopend
```

Figure 2.10

Practical exercise 2.1 _____

Copy the program template
B2:PORDINALS.TEXT, which the Course
Team have provided, on the block disk on
to your user disk and use the editor to
examine it. You will find a program body
implementing the design of Figure 2.10, but
the declarations part of the program is
missing.

(i)   Insert the **type** definitions and **var**
      declarations to complete the program.
(ii) The program that we have provided
      contains a few errors. By comparing the
      program with the design and examining
      the syntax, see if you can locate and
      correct these errors before attempting to
      compile it.
(iii) When you have successfully debugged
      the program compile and run it. Test
      the program by choosing a variety of
      data to test all options within the **case**
      construct.

You can check your program further by
looking at our solution in
B2:AORDINALS.TEXT.

2.4 Summary of section

An *enumeration type* is a *user-defined ordinal
type* in which the type definition lists all the
values which a variable of that type can
take. The format of the type definition is

type *identifier* = (*list of values*);

Variables of an enumeration type can be
declared and used in programs just like any
other variable.

Variables can be declared to be of an
enumeration type *implicitly* by a **var**
declaration of the form

var *identifier* : (*list of values*);

Confusion between *string* variables and
variables of an *enumeration type* is a
common source of programming errors.
string values *cannot* be assigned to
enumeration type variables, nor can they be
compared with values of an *enumeration
type* variable.

The use of enumeration type variables
enhances the readability of programs and is
helpful in confining the values of variables
to correct ranges of values.

3 Enumeration types and for loops

3.1 The ordering of enumeration types

The *ordinal* types *integer*, *char* and *Boolean* are ordered, so we can compare the values of variables of the *same* type using *relational operators* such as > and < = as we have seen already. Although it may not have been apparent from the work of the previous section, the *user-defined ordinal* type is also ordered; the ordering of an enumeration type is determined by the order in which the elements are listed in the type definition. So for example, with the **type** defined by

```
selection = (continue, stop, error);
```

continue is the first in order, *stop* the second and *error* third.

The expressions

```
continue < stop
error > = continue
```

both have value *true*.

SAQ 3.1

For the **type** definition

```
holidaymonth = (may, june, july, august,
                              september);
```

which of the following expressions take value *true*, and which *false*?

(i)   *june < august*
(ii) *september < = july*
(iii) (*june < july*) **or** (*may > august*)
(iv) (*may < june*) **and** (*september < = may*)

Solution 3.1

(i)   True
(ii) False
(iii) True
(iv) False

In the first example there is nothing natural about the ordering of the values of the type *selection*, and so it is difficult to see how this ordering could be at all helpful to us in program design. The ordering of the months from May to September looks more familiar, though to compare months using

relational operators is still somewhat contrived. But consider the design extract in Figure 3.1.

```
loop for month from May to September
    read in rainfallhours and sunshinehours
    calculate totalrain and totalsun
loopend
```

Figure 3.1

The designer has chosen to express the **for** loop in terms of familiar month names and it is implicit in this design that the loop will be executed five times, once for each of the months from May to September inclusive.

Until now we have only allowed variables of type *integer* as control variable in a **for** loop. So, how can we implement the design of Figure 3.1 in Pascal? Pascal allows *any* ordinal type to be used as a loop control variable. Consequently if we define *month* to be a variable of **type** *holidaymonth* then the design in Figure 3.1 is implemented as shown in Figure 3.2.

```
for month: = may to september do
    begin
        {repeated statements}
    end.
```

Figure 3.2

Notice that we chose to use lower case letters throughout for the identifiers in the definition of *holidaymonth*, in order to distinguish them from the names of the months as used in ordinary text. This is a point of detail, but what does matter in the definition is the order in which the identifiers were listed. If we had defined instead:

```
badmonths = (june, may, august, september, july)
```

this would be a perfectly valid enumeration type definition even though it is creating an unnatural ordering of the listed months. The loop control statement

```
for nextone: = may to september do
```

(where *nextone* is a variable of **type** *badmonths*) is a valid **for** statement, but the loop would be executed just three times, corresponding to the values *may*, *august* and *september* of *nextone*.

In attempting the next exercise, recall that we mentioned that **for** loops can be controlled by variables of *any* ordinal type, and that includes the **type** *char*.

Exercise 3.1 _____

Assuming the declarations in Figure 3.3.

```
type
    scale = (do, re, mi, fa, so, la, ti);
var
    i: integer;
    letter: char;
    note: scale;
    sex: (male, female);
```

Figure 3.3

decide which of the following **for** statements are valid, and for those which are valid determine how many times such a loop would be executed.

(i)   **for** note := re **to** fa **do**
(ii) **for** note := so **to** do **do**
(iii) **for** note := do **downto** re **do**
(iv) **for** i := '1' **to** '9' **do**
(v)   **for** letter := 'a' **to** 'z' **do**
(vi) **for** letter := 'A' **downto** 'A' **do**
(vii) **for** sex := male **to** female **do**

Practical exercise 3.1 _____

We have discussed the order of the character set giving some information about the relative positions of the lower and upper case letters and digits. A simple experiment will enable you to find for yourself where the various punctuation marks, and other characters occur in the ordering.

Type in the program in Figure 3.4.

```
program charorder;
var ch: char;
begin
    for ch := '0' to 'z' do {the '0' is the digit zero}
        write(ch)
end.
```

Figure 3.4

Compile and run the program.

All the characters from the digit *0* to the lower case *z* are listed in character order. You should notice, however, that there are many expected characters still missing; for example, the space character and round and curly brackets are not included. Experiment with different character values in the **for** statement to extend your enumeration of the character set.

3.2 Writing and reading enumeration types

In the previous section we mentioned that we cannot read in values of a variable of *enumeration type* from the keyboard, and neither can such a value be written out to screen or printer. Although values of *enumeration type* look like *strings*, they are *not strings* and Pascal does not allow them to be read and written like strings. There are, however, times when you want to input, or output, enumeration type values and this deficiency has to be overcome.

In Figure 3.1 we gave a design extract for a simple program to input the number of rain and sunshine hours for each month, and to total these amounts over a five month period. The program is not difficult to implement as you can see from Figure 3.5.

```
program holidayweather;
type holidaymonth = (may, june, july, august, september);
var month: holidaymonth;
    rainhours, sunhours, totalrain, totalsun: integer;
begin
    totalrain := 0;
    totalsun := 0; {initialize variables updated in loop}
    for month := may to september do
        begin
            readln(rainhours);
            totalrain := totalrain + rainhours;
            readln(sunhours);
            totalsun := totalsun + sunhours
        end;
    writeln('Total hours of rain = ',totalrain);
    writeln('Total hours of sun = ',totalsun)
end.
```

Figure 3.5

This program would perform as required, but a user might find it awkward because of the absence of prompts. We really want to prompt for the five pairs of integer inputs. There appears to be a simple solution. We could add the following statement to our program as the first line of the **for** loop, following the **begin**:

```
writeln('Input rain and sunshine hours for the month of ',month);
```

Unfortunately, this will not work because Pascal will not let us write the value of *month*, which is *not* of **type** *string*. One way around this is to use the code in Figure 3.6. This will result in the prompt that we want.

```
write('Input rain and sunshine hours for the month of');
case month of
    may        : writeln('May');
    june       : writeln('June');
    july       : writeln('July');
    august     : writeln('August');
    september : writeln('September')
end;
```

Figure 3.6

SAQ 3.2

Why have we used *write*, rather than *writeln*, in the first line of this code?

Solution 3.2

Using *write* will keep the whole prompt, including the month (which is written from the **case** statement), all on one line. Had we used *writeln*, the prompt would have been written on two lines:

> Input rain and sunshine hours for the month of
> July

The essence of the code in Figure 3.6 is that the values of the *enumeration type* variable *month* are being matched with corresponding *string* values, the latter of which can be written out. In the previous section we carried out a similar manoeuvre to set the value of a variable of enumeration type, which cannot be keyed-in. In the *ordinals* program we keyed-in an *integer* value of *score* which played a dual role. The value of the *enumeration type* variable *action* was assigned, by program statements, according to the input value of *score* using the conversion in the table in Figure 2.9.

Practical exercise 3.2

A company requires to know the average number of man-hours lost per day through absenteeism over a five day week. You are to assume that each employee works an 8 hour day and that the number of absentees for each day of the week, Monday to Friday, are to be input.

In designing your solution plan to use a **for** loop controlled by an *enumeration type* variable which takes five values, one for each of the days from Monday to Friday.

When your program is running the dialogue between the computer and the user should take the form shown in Figure 3.7.

A program template is not provided but

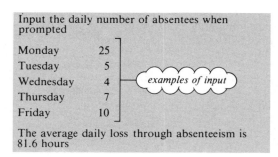

Figure 3.7

you can compare your program with the Course Team's solution on **B2:ABSENT.TEXT**.

3.3 Successor and predecessor

A **for** loop controlled by a variable of *enumeration type* works in just the same way as a **for** loop controlled by an *integer* variable.

The loop with control statement

```
for month := may to september do
```

initializes the value of *month* to may, and then increments the value of *month* at each completion of the sequence of statements within the loop. The loop is repeated until it completes the pass of the loop during which *month* has the final value *september*. What we mean by *increments* in this context is that the value of *month* is updated from its current value to the next value of the *enumeration type*. We have a name for the next value, not just of an enumeration type but of *any* ordinal type; it is called the **successor**. By analogy, when decrementing the values of an ordinal type, the previous value is known as the **predecessor**.

SAQ 3.3

For the enumeration type

```
spectrum = (red, orange, yellow, green, blue,
                          indigo, violet);
```

what is

(i)   The successor of *yellow*?

(ii) The predecessor of *indigo*?

(iii) The successor of *violet*?

Solution 3.3

(i)   *green*

(ii) *blue*

(iii) *violet* does not have a successor. It is the last value in the enumeration of *spectrum*.

Pascal provides a way of incrementing and decrementing values of *any* ordinal type by providing code which allows values to be updated to the *successor* and *predecessor* respectively.

If you have possessed a calculator then it would almost certainly have had some *function* keys. For example, it should have had a built-in routine for calculating the square-root of any positive number. Pascal, likewise, has a collection of standard, built-in functions. In *Unit 2* of the *next block* we shall introduce these functions, and also show how to define functions of our own invention. However, two of the standard functions which merit mention at this point are the functions *succ* and *pred*.

If *item* is a variable of an *ordinal* type then

succ(item) = the successor of the current value of *item*. It is undefined if the current value of *item* has no successor.

pred(item) = the predecessor of the current value of *item*. It is undefined if the current value of *item* has no predecessor.

So the line of code to increment a variable *colour* of **type** *spectrum* would be

```
colour: = succ(colour)
```

though this would result in a run-time error if *colour* already took the final value *violet*.

As an example of the use of *succ*, recall the program *choose_dealer* developed in the *previous* unit. There, the variable *player* was defined to be of **type** *integer* (though it only took values *1*, *2*, *3* and *4*), and the program fragment which selected the next player to receive a card was as shown in Figure 3.8.

```
if player = 4
then
    player: = 1
else
    player: = player + 1
```

Figure 3.8

Now if we adopt a more natural data type:

```
participant = (imogen, ken, peter, louise);
```

and declare *player* to be of **type** *participant*, then this same fragment of program would code as shown in Figure 3.9.

```
if player = louise
then
    player: = imogen
else
    player: = succ(player)
```

Figure 3.9

Exercise 3.2

In Figure 3.10 we have given most of a program whose purpose is to predict which day of the week a date in January 1988 falls on, given the 1st is a Friday. The user is to input any January day (1 to 31) and the program writes out on which day of the week this particular date falls.

Supply the two missing steps.

```
program find_day;
type days_of_week = (sun, mon, tues, wed, thur, fri, sat);
var day: days_of_week;
    current, search: integer;
begin
    writeln('Input day—from 1 to 31');
    readln(search);
    day: = thur;
    for current: = 1 to search do
        {update day}
    write('Day ', search:3, 'of January falls on a ')
        {write out day}
end.
```

Figure 3.10

If, in the above exercise, you supplied the code for updating day as simply

```
day: = succ(day);
```

then the program would compile but you would get a *run-time error* when a value of *search* exceeding 2 is input. The reason for this is that the line attempts to evaluate *succ(sat)* which is not defined. The fact that *sat* has no successor in *days_of_week* goes against our experience, for a Saturday is followed by a Sunday. Indeed the days of the week do not really form a linear structure going from a first in order to a last; they are 'cyclically ordered' as shown in Figure 3.11.

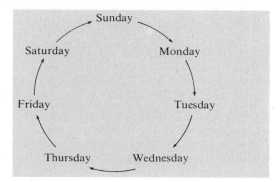

Figure 3.11

We have used enumeration types to represent other collections of data which have this cyclic ordering; for example, the traffic-light sequence, the notes of the scale and the four card players. In Pascal we have to represent these structures linearly, as an *enumeration type*, deciding on one element to be the first in order, thereby making its (natural) predecessor the last. We can use the successor function to step along the list as far as the last member, but we then need a step of code (as in Exercise 3.2) to mimic the first member succeeding the last.

SAQ 3.4 _____

Write the code that would take the variable *day* to its predecessor in *days_of_week*, including taking *sun* to *sat*.

Solution 3.4

```
if day = sun
then
    day:= sat
else
    day:= pred(day)
ifend
```

3.4 Summary of section

This section has been concerned with order in *ordinal data*. When an *enumeration type* is defined an ordering of the data values is defined by their listing.

The control variable in a **for** loop can be of *any ordinal type*. We have seen examples of **for** loops controlled by *character* variables and *enumeration type* variables.

The functions *succ* and *pred* can be used with *any ordinal data* respectively mapping a value to its successor and predecessor. A *run-time error* occurs if an attempt is made to evaluate the successor of the last member, or the predecessor of the first member, of an *ordinal type*.

4 *Other uses for ordinal data types*

4.1 Array indexing

In dealing with arrays, we have so far only used *integer* values for the indexes. In fact, arrays can be indexed using any ordinal type. For example, if we have defined the **type**

```
days_of_week = (sun, mon, tues, wed, thur, fri,
                                              sat);
```

then we can also define the *array* **type**

```
workhours = array[days_of_week] of integer;
```

A variable *daytotal* of **type** *workhours* will then be an array with seven elements, each of which (after initialization) holds an *integer* value as shown in Figure 4.1.

array	346	— daytotal[sun]
daytotal	123	— daytotal[mon]
	94	— daytotal[tues]
	87	— daytotal[wed]
	88	— daytotal[thur]
	149	— daytotal[fri]
	193	— daytotal[sat]

Figure 4.1

We can then employ the *ordinal type index* in, for example, **for** loops. The program fragment in Figure 4.2 adds up the seven *integer* values in the above array, where the loop control variable *day* is of **type** *days_of_week*.

```
weektotal := 0;
for day := sun to sat do
begin
    weektotal := weektotal + daytotal[day]
end;
```

Figure 4.2

Exercise 4.1 _____

The table in Figure 4.3 gives rainfall figures to the nearest millimetre, collated monthly over a period of one year.

Jan	Feb	Mar	Apr	May	Jun	Jul	Aug	Sep	Oct	Nov	Dec
35	43	29	32	17	8	5	6	11	17	27	23

Figure 4.3

(i)   Declare a suitable array to hold this data using the *enumeration type*

```
month = (jan, feb, mar, apr, may, jun, jul, aug, sep, oct, nov, dec);
```

(ii) What is the index of the month with 32 mm of rain?

(iii) Write a fragment of program to add up the total rainfall over the period from May to September.

As with *enumeration types*, inclusion of the **type** definition is not mandatory, for it can be made implicitly in a **var** declaration. For instance,

```
var daytotal: array[days_of_week] of integer;
```

declares *daytotal* to be a variable of the unnamed **type array**[*days_of_week*] **of** *integer*.

When using *integers* as the index of an array the *size* of the array has to be stipulated by a *subrange* of the set of integers. For example we may have **types**:

```
array[1..12] of string;  or
array[−5..5] of real;
```

In the same way we can use subranges of any ordinal type for the index set of an array. To focus on weekdays alone, we take the subrange mon..fri of the *enumeration type days_of_week*. So in a program where the **type** *days_of_week* is defined we can also define the **type**

```
array[mon..fri] of real;
```

which would be an array of five elements, indexed by mon to fri inclusive, and base **type** *real*.

The one important rule to remember in connection with subranges is that the second listed member *must not* come before the first listed member in the type order.

SAQ 4.1

Assuming that the **type**

> spectrum = (red, orange, yellow, green, blue, indigo, violet);

has been defined, which of the following are valid types:

(i) **array**[orange..blue] **of** integer;

(ii) **array**[spectrum] **of** spectrum;

(iii) **array**[red..violet] **of** char;

(iv) **array**[indigo..green] **of** real;

(v) **array**[red..blue] **of array**[1..12] **of** integer;

(vi) **array**['a'..'z'] **of** integer;

(vii) **array**[integer] **of** spectrum;

Solution 4.1

(i) valid. This array has four elements of base type integer.

(ii) valid. This array has seven elements of base type spectrum. The base type of an array can be any type.

(iii) valid. The same array could be declared as **array**[spectrum] **of** char.

(iv) invalid. There are no elements in indigo..green since green comes before indigo in spectrum order.

(v) valid. This is an array with five elements whose values are arrays with twelve elements (or a two-dimensional array which is explained later).

(vi) valid. The characters form an ordinal set within which the subrange 'a'..'z' contains 26 elements. So this is an array of base type integer, indexed by the 26 lower case letters.

(vii) invalid. We cannot index an array by the infinite set of all integers. A finite subrange must be specified.

4.2 Currency exchange, revisited

In *Unit 1* of this block, one of the examples that we used to illustrate the use of parallel arrays involved currency exchange rates. Figure 4.4 contains these exchange rates and the name of each currency.

With the enumeration type now available, let us define the **type**

> countries = (austria, belgium, canada, france, greece, italy, portugal, spain, switzerland, usa, wgermany, yugoslavia);

We can hold the exchange rates and currencies in arrays indexed appropriately by the corresponding country.

country	rate	currency
Austria	22.40	schilling
Belgium	65.70	bfranc
Canada	2.08	cdollar
France	9.85	ffranc
Greece	223.00	drachma
Italy	2170.00	lira
Portugal	210.00	escudo
Spain	200.00	peseta
Switzerland	2.68	sfranc
USA	1.46	usdollar
W. Germany	3.19	dmark
Yugoslavia	460.00	dinar

Figure 4.4

> **var**
> rate: **array**[countries] **of** real;
> currency: **array**[countries] **of** string;

SAQ 4.2

What are the values of

(i) rate[france],   (ii) rate[usa],

(iii) currency[yugoslavia]?

Solution 4.2

(i) 9.85,   (ii) 1.46,   (iii) dinar

We are now going to write a program which uses this currency exchange information. Suppose that the computer holds the information from Figure 4.4 in the two arrays rate and currency as defined above. The purpose of our program is to receive one of the twelve listed currencies along with a specified number of pounds as input from the user, and to inform the user how much of the currency she would receive in exchange. A typical dialogue might be as shown in Figure 4.5.

> Which currency do you want? dinar
> How many pounds do you wish to exchange? 150
> £150 are worth 69000.00 dinar

Figure 4.5

In Figure 4.6 we have given a top-level design of a solution to this problem.

```
1   initialize arrays
2   read in currency wanted
3   read in number of pounds
4   calculate exchange value
5   write out exchange value
```

Figure 4.6

The refinement of step 1 is routine, though somewhat tedious. We have to set 24 values, 12 for each of the two arrays given in Figure 4.4. The arrays *rate* and *currency* constitute the main data in the problem, but before attempting refinement of the other steps we shall introduce some of the other variables which are needed. Figure 4.7 contains a data table for the problem.

The conversion from pounds to a specified currency looks straightforward; we simply multiply the number of pounds by the appropriate exchange rate.

SAQ 4.3 _____

Refine step 4.

Solution 4.3

| 4.1 | set exchange to amount * rate[destination] |

The step which is going to require careful refinement is step 2. We are envisaging the user keying in a string value for the currency requested. The program is going to have to recognize this string as one of the twelve currencies, so that it can assign the appropriate value to *destination* (the variable for the country whose currency is required), as required in step 4. (A better program design would offer the user a 'menu' of available currencies from which she could select without typing in the name. We shall introduce such menus in *Block III*.)

To cater for erroneous inputs we shall embed the *read* statement in a loop which repeats until a correct string is input. So step 2 refines as shown in Figure 4.8.

Exercise 4.2 _____

A simple way of checking whether or not *wanted* is a valid currency is to scan the list of all currencies checking *wanted* against each in turn. We shall use a *Boolean* variable *valid* to indicate success of the search; *valid* is initially *false* and set *true* only if *wanted* is found. Refine step 2.3 in this way.

Our final design is now shown in Figure 4.9. Note that the use of a **for** loop in this situation is not necessarily the most efficient way, but it has the advantage of simplicity.

Identifier	Description	Type
rate	array holding exchange rates	array[countries] of real variable
currency	array holding currency names	array[countries] of string variable
wanted	required currency	string variable
amount	number of pounds to exchange	integer variable
destination	country whose currency is required	variable of type countries
exchange	value of exchange (i.e. the amount) in the foreign currency	real variable
country	for indexing arrays rate and currency	variable of type countries

Figure 4.7

2.1	loop
2.2	read in wanted {the required currency}
2.3	check if wanted is a valid currency
2.4	until wanted is valid
2.5	loopend

Figure 4.8

Practical exercise 4.1 _____

In this exercise we ask you to implement the design of Figure 4.9. To help you with the amount of typing involved we have provided a program template which defines the *enumeration type* countries, and implements step 1 of the design by providing the statements to initialize the arrays *rate* and *currency*.

1	initialize arrays
2.1	loop
2.2	read in wanted
2.3.1	set valid to false
2.3.2	loop for all countries
2.3.3	if currency[country] = wanted
2.3.4	then
2.3.5	set valid to true
2.3.6	set destination to country of wanted
2.3.7	else
2.3.8	do nothing
2.3.9	ifend
2.3.10	loopend
2.4	until valid
2.5	loopend
3.1	read in amount
4.1	set exchange to amount * rate[destination]
5.1	write out exchange

Figure 4.9

Now, transfer the program template **B2:PCURREXCH.TEXT** to your user disk. Insert the rest of the code and compile the program. Run your program using a variety of test data, including invalid currency names. You may compare your program with the one provided by the Course Team, **B2:ACURREXCH.TEXT**.

4.3 Subrange types

We have met the idea of subranges through indexing arrays. A subrange is any collection of successive ordinals *integer*, *char*, *Boolean* or of *enumeration type*. As we mentioned with arrays, the only restriction is that the first value specifying the subrange must be less than or equal to the second value in the ordering of the type. Any subrange can be defined as a type. Thus we can have the examples shown in Figure 4.10.

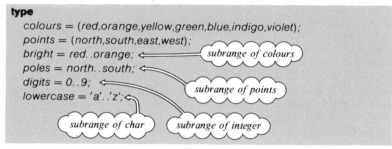

```
type
    colours = (red,orange,yellow,green,blue,indigo,violet);
    points = (north,south,east,west);
    bright = red..orange;     ← subrange of colours
    poles = north..south;     ←
    digits = 0..9;            ← subrange of points
    lowercase = 'a'..'z';     ←
                    subrange of char    subrange of integer
```

Figure 4.10

As with enumeration types, the subrange type identifier is not mandatory, for subranges can be defined implicitly. For example, with the **type** *colours* defined we can declare

```
var
    housecount: array[red..blue] of integer;
    surnamecount: array['A'..'Z'] of integer;
```

These valid declarations involve implicit subranges *red..blue* of *colours* and *'A'..'Z'* of the *standard ordinal* **type** *char*.

SAQ 4.4

Which of the following are valid subrange type definitions, where the **type** *colours* is defined as in Figure 4.10.

(i)   *punctuation = '*'..'}';*
(ii)   *litmus = blue..red;*
(iii) *surnames = 'aaa'..'zzz';*
(iv)   *players = 1..4;*

Solution 4.4

(i)   valid '*' comes before '}' in the ordering of the character set. *punctuation* is a valid subrange—even though the name might be inappropriate!
(ii)   invalid. *blue* is after *red* in *colours* order.
(iii) invalid. The underlying type is *string* which is not ordinal.
(iv)   valid. A subrange of *integer*.

The main benefit to be gained from using subranges is that a check is made automatically at run-time to ensure that the values assigned to variables of such subranges fall within the specified range. If an attempt is made to assign a value outside the range a run-time error will result. So, for example, if we were involved in a program which collated and analysed examination scores which were percentages, we would naturally define

```
type
    percentages = 0..100;
```

If an integer value outside this subrange was keyed in during the reading in of values of a variable of **type** *percentages*, an error would be reported instantly.

SAQ 4.5

Declare (using *implicit* type definitions) appropriate variables to represent

(i)   The temperature of water.
(ii)   The points accumulated by Arsenal over a football season.
(iii) The years in the 20th century.

Solution 4.5

(i)   *temperature: 0..100;* (or *32..212* if you think in Fahrenheit)
(ii)   *points: 0..126;*
(iii) *year: 1900..1999;*

Defined subranges are allowed to overlap. For example, the following **type** definitions are acceptable.

```
type
    percentages = 0..100;
    passes = 36..100;
```

This illustrates the difference between implicit type definitions and enumeration types. In enumeration types we have said that a value can only belong to one type. However, when dealing with overlapping subranges care must be taken with the use of assignment statements. For example, suppose that following the previous **type** definitions we now declare:

```
var
    score: percentages;
    gradeA: passes;
```

Now, consider the assignment

```
score:= gradeA
```

Strictly speaking, the assignment should be invalid because the variables involved are of different types. However, since both have the same underlying type *integer*, such assignments are permitted. What is more, since every value that *gradeA* can take lies in the subrange of *percentages*, the assignment is always sensible. The situation is similar to the one in which *integer* values can be assigned to a *real* variable. We say that such assignments are *assignment compatible*.

In contrast, the assignment

```
gradeA:= score
```

is not assignment compatible, because score may take values which are outside the subrange of values for *gradeA*.

Assignments which are not assignment compatible will compile but may lead to run-time errors.

4.4 Summary of section

Any *ordinal type* may be used for indexing an array. In this section we have seen examples of arrays indexed by values of an enumeration type and by characters.

Any collection of successive ordinals forms a *subrange* of that ordinal type. In the same way that arrays are indexed by a subrange of integer type, we can use subranges of ordinal type.

Subranges can be defined as types. One benefit of doing this is to confine the values of variables to appropriate ranges with an in-built check against erroneous values.

5 Multi-dimensional arrays

5.1 Two-dimensional arrays

By now you should be becoming confident in the handling of one-dimensional arrays, using a single identifier to hold a list of values of the same type, where each individual value is identified by an associated index. In the examples that we have met so far, the values in question (that is, the *base type* of the array) have been *real*, *integer*, *character* or *string*. However, the base type of an array in Pascal can be *any* type (except file type, which we shall meet in *Block V*). In SAQ 4.1 we indicated that the base type of an array might itself be an array—an array of arrays! We shall explore this notion in this section.

Let us look at an example. Suppose that we have the declaration

> **var**
> *example*: **array**[1..6] **of array**[1..4] **of** *integer;*

How can we visualise such a structure? *example* is an array indexed by the subrange *1..6* of *integer*, and so the array has six elements as shown in Figure 5.1.

| example[1] |
| example[2] |
| example[3] |
| example[4] |
| example[5] |
| example[6] |

Figure 5.1

Now each of these array elements is itself an array; it is an array indexed by *1..4* and having base type *integer*. So we can picture example as shown in Figure 5.2, where we have inserted possible values into the twenty-four cells.

As *example[1]* is an array indexed from 1 to 4, it has the four elements:

| example[1] [1] | example[1] [2] | example[1] [3] | example[1] [4] |

In general, the element of *example[i]* with index *j* has identifier

> *example[i] [j]*

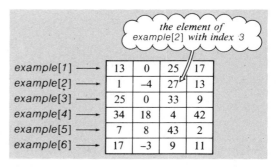

Figure 5.2

SAQ 5.1 _____

(i) With the value of *example* given in Figure 5.2, write down the values of *example[2] [1]*, *example[1] [2]* and *example[5] [3]*

(ii) Write down the identifiers for the elements of example which have values 7 and −4.

Solution 5.1
(i) 1, 0, 43
(ii) example[5] [1], example[2] [2].

A one-dimensional array whose elements are themselves one-dimensional arrays is called a **two-dimensional array**, and we have a notation which allows us to avoid talking about arrays of arrays. The array *example* is a *two-dimensional array* and it can also be declared by the statement

> **var**
> *example*: **array**[1..6, 1..4] **of** *integer;*

With this improved notation the indexing of the elements works in exactly the same way as before, but looks slightly different. The element which we identified previously as *example[i] [j]* is, in the revised notation, element *example[i, j]*.

SAQ 5.2 _____

Suppose we declare

> **var**
> *example*: **array**[1..6, 1..4] **of** *integer;*

and *example* has the values as shown in

Figure 5.2. Write down

(i) The values of *example*[2, 4] and *example*[5, 2]

(ii) The identifiers of the elements which have values −3 and 43.

Solution 5.2

(i) 13, 8

(ii) *example*[6, 2] and *example*[5, 3].

Whenever we have a two-dimensional table of data in which all the entries are of the same base type, then the structure can be represented by a two-dimensional array. For example, a league table consisting of five columns of integers headed as shown in Figure 5.3.

played	won	draw	lost	points

Figure 5.3

With a row for each of twenty-two teams, it could be held in an array of:

type
    table = **array**[1..22, 1..5] **of** *integer;*

Exercise 5.1 _____

(i) A page is to consist of 120 lines, each line comprising a maximum of 66 characters. Define a suitable type for the variable *page*.

(ii) In a survey of visitors to an exibition the sex and age (in one of six bands: <21, 21–30, 31–40, 41–50, 51–60, >60) of each individual was recorded. The total for each of the twelve categories was entered as data into the computer. Suggest a suitable data type for this structure.

5.2 Using two-dimensional arrays

From the few examples of two-dimensional arrays that we have now met you will probably realize that they are a naturally occurring structure, and consequently we shall make considerable use of them. Most of what we shall do with two-dimensional arrays concerns storing and retrieving information, and will involve ideas that we have already encountered with one-dimensional arrays. The major difference is that the elements of the array are accessed via two indexes, rather than one, and we must get used to navigating around arrays using the pair of indexes.

Let us look at an example. An Open University Examination Board has maintained the results for its course in an array

    results: **array**[1976..1986, 1..6] **of** *integer;*

For each year the marks of all students who took the course are classified and recorded according to six categories. The categories are: four pass grades (1 to 4), fail (5) and drop out (6). The array *results* can be pictured as a rectangular array, with eleven rows indexed 1976 to 1986 inclusive, and six columns indexed 1 to 6 as shown in Figure 5.4.

indexes	1	2	3	4	5	6
1976	96	103	84	76	31	43
1977	101	127	119	101	29	38
1978	121	134	130	119	36	34
1979	113	143	127	95	46	51
1980	96	117	110	91	39	60
1981	93	121	97	103	31	46
1982	86	109	101	91	26	39
1983	97	111	115	99	23	41
1984	81	97	93	87	24	56
1985	79	86	91	98	29	49
1986	85	101	87	94	22	39

Figure 5.4

So *results*[i, j] represents the number of students in year i who were awarded category j. Using our picture of the 11 by 6 rectangular array, the value of *results*[i, j] will be found at the intersection of row i and column j.

The following exercise examines your understanding of the roles of the two indexes.

Exercise 5.2 _____

Suppose that the array *results* had been initialized.

(i) Write a fragment of program to count the total number of students who embarked on the course in 1980.

(ii) Write a fragment of program to determine the average number of students being awarded pass grade 1 over the eleven-year period.

So, with our picture of results as being a rectangular array, we can scan any row by setting that row index and looping over the full range of column indexes. Similarly, we can scan any column by setting the column index and looping over the full range of row indexes. But how do we scan the whole of the two-dimensional array? What we must do is to take our algorithm for scanning a row and repeat it in a loop which takes in all the rows. The Pascal implementation would be as shown in Figure 5.5.

```
for row:= 1976 to 1986 do
   begin
      for col:= 1 to 6 do
         begin
            {repeated statements involving results[row, col]}
         end {for col}
   end {for row}
```

Figure 5.5

where *row* and *col* are declared as *integer* (or appropriate subrange) variables.

SAQ 5.3 _____

Write a program fragment which adds up the total number of students who have embarked on this course over the eleven-year period.

Solution 5.3

```
sum:= 0; {initialize count}
for row:= 1976 to 1986 do
   begin
      for col:= 1 to 6 do
         begin
            sum:= sum + results[row, col]
         end
   end
```

Figure 5.6

In each of the above examples we scan the whole array in the way depicted in Figure 5.7 (i); the outer loop selects each row index in turn and, for each row index, the inner

loop then takes us through each column. We refer to this as a row scan of the array. Figure 5.7 (ii) shows the alternative column scan.

SAQ 5.4 _____

How do you modify the Solution to SAQ 5.3 so that the elements of the array are summed in column scan order?

Solution 5.4

Interchange the two **for** statements. The inner loop then sums the array entries down the current value of column and the outer loop repeats this for the full range of values of *col*.

5.3 Searching two-dimensional arrays

Having discussed one-dimensional arrays in *Unit 1* of this block we went on in *Unit 2* to spend a good deal of time developing a variety of algorithms to search them for given values. You might, therefore, be anticipating a long discourse on searching two-dimensional arrays. However, this is not to be, and for one very good reason. The clever searching algorithms that we developed all hinged around the fact that the one-dimensional array was ordered. For arrays that are not ordered, we can do no better than just scan the whole array.

Now, many of the data collections that we represented by a one-dimensional array were naturally ordered; integer values in ascending order, names in alphabetical order, and so on. However, the structures that are naturally represented by two-dimensional arrays are tables of data for which there is no real ordering as such. What do we mean by saying that a table is ordered?

The gist of these remarks is that the only practical way of searching two-dimensional arrays for given values is by traversing the whole array, either by row scan or column scan.

Exercise 5.3 _____

Design an algorithm for searching a two-dimensional array called *items*, of base type *string*, for a particular value *searchstring*, which may or may not be present. The algorithm must report the presence or otherwise, and if present determine the two indexes (called *row* and *col*) pinpointing the position of *searchstring* in *items*.

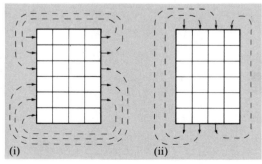

(i)   (ii)

Figure 5.7

5.4 Higher dimensions

As the base type of an array can be any type, we can define types which are arrays of two-dimensional arrays, that is, three-dimensional arrays. With three-dimensional arrays as the base type of an array we get four-dimensional arrays, and so on. The type definitions are a straightforward extension of the two-dimensional case. For example,

```
var
    cube: array[1..4, 1..4, 1..4] of char;
```

declares a variable *cube* which is a three-dimensional array, with a total of 64 elements, with base type *char*. We can visualize the structure as a $4 \times 4 \times 4$ cube, with each of the 64 sub-cubes holding a character value. The values are accessed via three indexes each taking values in the range 1 to 4 inclusive, such as *cube*[2, 4, 1].

SAQ 5.5 _____

From a survey in which 1000 teenagers were asked how many hours of television they watch per day on average (to the nearest whole hour), the data was stored in an array

```
survey: array[13..19, sex, 0..8] of integer;
```

where the

```
type sex = (male, female);
```

has been defined.

(i)   How many values does the array *survey* hold?

(ii) How would you interpret the value found in *survey*[18, male, 0]?

(iii) Where would you find the number of 15 year old girls who watch 4 hours of television?

Solution 5.5

(i) $7 \times 2 \times 9 = 126$

(ii) This is the number of 18 year old boys who claim to watch no television.

(iii) *survey*[15, female, 4]

Exercise 5.4 _____

Write a design for a program based on the array *survey* in SAQ 5.5, which:

(i)   Determines the percentage of teenagers who watch at least 3 hours of television per day.

(ii) Counts how many boys watch not more than 2 hours of television per day.

(iii) Counts how many 15 year old girls were involved in the survey.

5.5 Summary of section

Two-dimensional arrays are used to hold a variety of collections of data which resemble tables of values of the *same* type. The array type can be defined either implicitly in a **var** declaration, or as a **type** definition of the form:

```
type
    arraytype = array[range1, range2] of base type;
```

where *range1* and *range2* are any subranges of ordinal type.

Elements of a two-dimensional array are accessed by use of two indexes, the first pinpointing a value in *range1* and the second a value in *range2*, with notation *example*[*index1*, *index2*] (where *example* is of *arraytype*).

Two-dimensional arrays can be searched by row scan or column scan. These ideas can be extended to higher dimensions. Three-dimensional arrays have three subranges in the type definition, and accordingly require three indexes to access the elements.

6 *A practical example*

6.1 The results analysis problem

In this section we are going to design and implement a solution to a relatively complex problem involving a two-dimensional array. The problem that we are going to investigate is a familiar one. A class teacher keeps examination results by recording in a table the marks (as percentages) gained by each pupil in his class for each subject. The left-hand top corner of the results table may well look like Figure 6.1.

	Maths	Latin	French	History
A. Allen	64	33	58	46
M. Allsop	57	39	56	54
E. Baker	73	59	68	83
C. Bamforth	60	37	48	

Figure 6.1

The teacher wishes to put this data onto a computer and from it to determine the average mark attained by each pupil. Further, from descending order of average marks, he wants the pupils placed in rank order in the class.

Do we understand the problem? Well, not fully. Are all the pupils to take the same set of subjects? And what happens if, through absence or some other reason, a pupil has no mark for a certain subject? A simple design decision will enable us to surmount both these difficulties. We shall assume that a pupil cannot get a genuine mark of 0 and so reserve the recorded mark 0 to signify that no mark is available for that pupil in that subject. When we come to work out averages we must remember that 0s are to be ignored.

6.2 Selecting data structures

The next step, before we consider algorithms to solve the problem, is to decide which data structure we should use

to hold the data. This decision is central to the problem. We have a table of integer values and our design decision has ensured no gaps; non-marks are recorded as 0. The rows of the table correspond to pupils and the columns to subjects. That cries out for an appropriate two-dimensional array, but how big is it? We are not told how many pupils or how many subjects there are. To overcome these problems we could employ two *integer constants*; *classize* for the number of pupils and *numberofsubjects* for the number of subjects. For each application of our eventual program appropriate values for these constants will have to be declared.

SAQ 6.1 _____

Declare a variable *marks* to hold the *table* of values.

Solution 6.1

```
type
    table = array[1..classize, 1..numberofsubjects] of 0..100;
var
    marks: table;
```

By starting to enumerate the pupils and the subjects in Figure 6.1 we were hinting at labelling the rows and columns of the table by values of an enumeration type. Indeed, references such as *marks[E.Baker, latin]* are far more meaningful than *marks[3, 2]*. But listing all the pupil names as an enumeration type creates one drawback. Our program will inevitably have to 'loop for all pupils' and to code this would require the first and last pupil names:

```
for student:= A.Allen to B.Wilson do
```

As specific names then appear in the program body, our program would be applicable to just this one class of students. To preserve generality we must use the integer index for pupils.

On the other hand it makes more sense to use an *enumeration type* for the subjects. The subject lists are fairly standard and our program body will only need the first and the last (so that we can 'loop for all subjects'). We shall, therefore, use an enumeration type and fix the first listed subject to be Maths, and the last English.

Solution 6.1 (Improved)

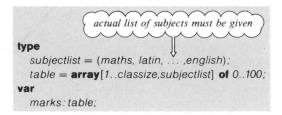

```
type
    subjectlist = (maths, latin, ... ,english);
    table = array[1..classize,subjectlist] of 0..100;
var
    marks: table;
```

To decode from *marks[5, french]* which student has scored this number of marks in French, we need the identity of pupil number 5. To achieve this we must list the pupil names in an array which is parallel to the rows of the table marks. The situation is depicted in Figure 6.2.

So we shall hold the pupil names in an array declared by

```
var
    pupil: array[1..classize] of string;
```

SAQ 6.2

(i) Which pupil has score
     marks[8, chemistry] ?
(ii) Where will we find the mark in
     geography attained by *pupil[5]* ?

Solution 6.2

(i) *pupil[8]*
(ii) *marks[5, geography]*

Having selected the data structures to hold the given information, we must now turn to the results of our computations. We are to compute the average mark for each pupil and, from the pupil's average marks, determine a rank ordering for the class. This will require two further arrays; one to hold the overall average marks (*overall*) and one to hold each pupil's class position (*rank*). These arrays will have one element per pupil and so will be in parallel with the rows of the array marks. Figure 6.3 shows the array structure pictorially.

At this point we shall make one further design decision. The base type of the array *overall* should, in principle, be *real*. However, we shall decide to round each pupil's average percentage mark to the nearest whole number, as is often done in practice. So, *overall* will contain *integer* values.

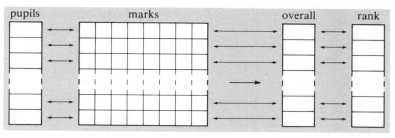

Figure 6.2

Figure 6.3

Exercise 6.1

Supply the missing type entries in the provisional data table in Figure 6.4.

Identifier	Description	Type
classize	total number of pupils	?
marks	array holding all the pupil marks for each subject	?
pupil	array of pupil names	?
overall	array holding each pupil's overall average mark	?
rank	array holding each pupil's rank position in class	?
subject	a control variable for looping through subjects	?
classno	a control variable for looping through pupils	?

Figure 6.4

Although it may seem to you that we are making little headway towards solving the problem set, we have, on the contrary, taken a big step in that direction. Selection of the data structures and main variables to be used in the solution of a problem is a key step in the solution process. Now we must turn to the program design.

6.3 A design solution

In terms of the pictorial representation of the problem in Figure 6.3, we are to be given (or to read in) the data in the arrays on the left of the figure (i.e. *marks* and *pupil*) and our primary task is to compute the data filling the arrays on the right (i.e.

overall and *rank*). Finally, we have to present our results in some appropriate fashion. The problem clearly breaks up into four parts which we reflect in our top-level solution in Figure 6.5.

```
1   initialize arrays
2   determine averages
3   determine rank order
4   write out results
```

Figure 6.5

Step 2 involves scanning each row (pupil) of the *marks* array and calculating the average by dividing the sum of all the marks by the total number of marks (remembering to discount any 0s). This number is then rounded and recorded in the appropriate entry of the array *overall*. A first refinement of step 2 is shown in Figure 6.6.

```
2.1   loop for all pupils
2.2      calculate rounded average mark
2.3      record mark
2.4   loopend
```

Figure 6.6

Exercise 6.2

Refine steps 2.2 and 2.3 and draw up a data table for any new variables that you use.

We have presented a refinement of step 3 in Figure 6.7. Have a quick look through it now and then read the commentary that follows.

```
3.1    set top to highest average mark
3.2    set position to 1
3.3    loop
3.4       set count to 0
3.5       loop for all pupils
3.6          if average = top
3.7          then
3.8             set rank to position
3.9             increment count
3.10         else
3.11            do nothing
3.12         ifend
3.13      loopend
3.14      decrement top
3.15      set position to position + count
3.16   until all positions allocated
3.17   loopend
```

Figure 6.7

Steps 3.1 and 3.2 initialize two variables. The variable *top* is set equal to the highest average mark for the class, and the variable *position* is set to 1. The inner loop, steps 3.5

to 3.13, scans the array *overall* searching for *average* marks equal to (the current value of) *top*. For any that are found the corresponding value of *rank* is set to (the current value of) *position*. After each pass of the inner loop the variables *top* and *position* are updated (steps 3.14 and 3.15). *top* is decreased by 1. Note that if, say, 3 pupils with the same average mark are all allocated position 5 in class, then the next value of *position* is 8. The variable *count* is used for this purpose, counting the number of pupils with the same average mark, being set to 0 prior to the inner loop and incremented within it. The outer loop (steps 3.3 to 3.17) is repeated until (at step 3.16) all positions have been allocated.

SAQ 6.3

The only steps in this refinement of step 3 which require further refinement are 3.1 and 3.16.

(i) Refine step 3.1.
(ii) What will the value of *position* be when all class positions have been allocated? Use this to refine step 3.16.

Solution 6.3

(i)
```
3.1.1   set top to 0
3.1.2   loop for all pupils
3.1.3      if average > top
3.1.4      then
3.1.5         set top to average
3.1.6      else
3.1.7         do nothing
3.1.8      ifend
3.1.9   loopend
```

Figure 6.8

(ii) When all positions are allocated the value of *position* will be *classize + 1*.

```
3.16.1   until position > classize
```

Steps 1 and 4 remain to be refined. Step 1 is straightforward, 'though somewhat tedious; we must assign initial values to a large number of variables. When we come to implement the program we shall provide you with the initialized arrays and consequently there is no need to refine this step of our design.

For step 4 we must decide how the results are to be presented. Let us suppose that the results are required in the form of pupil reports. For each pupil we are to display name, a list of marks for each subject, an overall average mark and a class position.

SAQ 6.4

Refine step 4.

Solution 6.4

```
4.1   loop for each pupil
4.2       write out name
4.3       loop for each subject
4.4           write out subject name
4.5           write out mark
4.6       loopend
4.7       write out overall average
4.8       write out class position
4.9   loopend
```

Figure 6.9

6.4 Implementing the solution

The design solution which we have now reached, when the four separately refined parts are put together, is as far as we need go before attempting to implement the solution. However, in our refinement of steps 2 and 3 we have introduced new variables which were not anticipated in our provisional data table in Figure 6.4. So let us first collate the additional items. Figure 6.10 contains a supplementary data table.

Identifier	Description	Type
sum	aggregate of pupil's marks	integer variable
number	number of subjects taken by pupil	integer variable
count	number of pupils with the same overall average	variable of subrange type 0..classize
mean	pupil's overall average mark	real variable
top	the next highest average during rank search	integer variable
average	pupil's rounded average mark	variable of subrange type 0..100
position	the next position in rank order	variable of subrange type 1..classize + 1

Figure 6.10

As far as implementation of our design is concerned, notice how the four steps can be coded independently, once we have agreed on identifiers of variables. Four separate fragments of code should run together to constitute the complete program. Step 3 should not cause any difficulty, so let us begin there.

Exercise 6.3

Write the code to implement the design in Figures 6.7 and 6.8.

Looking back to Figure 6.9, it looks at first sight as if implementation of step 4 is elementary, but there is one catch.

SAQ 6.5

Write the Pascal code for step 4.

Solution 6.5

The problem concerns step 4.4. As values of an enumeration type *cannot* be 'written out' we shall have to employ a **case** statement to select an appropriate *constant string* for each subject as is shown in Figure 6.11.

```
for classno := 1 to classize do
  begin
    writeln;
    writeln(pupil[classno]);
    writeln;
    for subject := maths to english do
      begin
        case subject of
          maths: write('Maths ');
          latin: write('Latin ');
              . . .
          english: write('English ')
        end; {of case}
        writeln(marks[classno, subject])
      end;
    writeln('Overall average = ', overall[classno]);
    writeln('Position in class = ', rank[classno])
  end;
```

Figure 6.11

Of course, a full enumeration of the subjects will be needed to complete this fragment of code!

In the coding of step 2 you will encounter a new feature; you have to 'round' a *real* number. As rounding is required so frequently in programming, Pascal provides a quick way of doing it. If *mean* is a real variable then the statement

```
average := round(mean)
```

assigns to the *integer* variable *average* the rounded value of *mean*.

(*round* is a standard Pascal function like *succ* and *pred* which you met in *Section 3.3* of this unit.)

Exercise 6.4

Now write the code for step 2 referring to the design in the solution of Exercise 6.2. (No solution to this exercise is given in the text, but you can look at the Course Team's complete program when you have finished the practical exercise that follows.)

Practical exercise 6.1 _____

In this exercise we want you to supply the missing code which implements step 2, that is, your answer to Exercise 6.4. As the overall program is quite long we have, as usual, eased your task by providing a substantial portion of it in a program template, **B2:PPUPILS.TEXT**. When you examine our template in the editor, you will notice that the arrays are initialized (step 1 of our design) by a single statement:

initialize(marks, pupil);

This calls up a separate piece of program provided by the Course Team in a Pascal unit, **B2:UPUPILS.CODE**. The program statement which tells the compiler that we are borrowing a unit:

uses {$u upupils.code} upupils;

is found immediately after the program heading. (We remind you that we do not expect you to understand how this borrowing of other bits of code works until you have studied *Block III*.)

Before starting the exercise transfer the program template **B2:PPUPILS.TEXT** and the unit **B2:UPUPILS.CODE** to your user disk. Insert the missing code, compile and execute your program.

If your program works correctly B.WILSON should finish 7th in the class with an average mark of 56.

You can examine our version of the completed program in **B2:APUPILS.TEXT**.

6.5 Summary of section

In this section we have solved a relatively complex problem. Our solution hinged around a two-dimensional array with an enumeration type as one of its indexes. In addition to providing more useful practice in problem solving, the section is intended as one for review and consolidation of the ideas introduced in the earlier sections of this unit.

Summary of unit

The principal purpose of this unit has been to introduce three new data types, examine their uses and limitations, and work through a variety of examples and situations involving them. The three types are:

(i) The *enumeration type*. When a variable in a problem is confined to taking only a small set of values which can feasibly be listed, Pascal allows the definition of an *abstract* type consisting of the listed set of values.

The definition takes the form

type
  type_identifier = (list of values);

where each value in the list conforms to the rules for an identifier.

The enumeration type is *ordinal*, the order being determined by the listing of the values. Enumeration types are used as a more natural representation of data in some problems, and their use can greatly improve the readability of programs.

(ii) The *subrange type*. Pascal allows *any* collection of consecutive values of *any* ordinal type to be defined as a subrange type. The type definition simply specifies the lower and upper values of the range:

type
  type_identifier = lowerbound..upperbound;

where lowerbound and upperbound are values of the *same* standard ordinal type or of a previously defined enumeration type.

Subrange types are used extensively for the indexing of arrays. They are also used to restrict values of variables to confined ranges.

(iii) The *two-dimensional array type*. An array whose elements are themselves arrays is called a two-dimensional array. Rather than talk of an array of arrays we think of a two-dimensional array as being a rectangular array, indexed by *two subranges*. The type definition takes the form

type
  type_identifier = **array**[*subrange1, subrange2*] **of** *base type;*

Two-dimensional arrays are the natural way of representing tables of data where all entries are of the *same* base type.

Solutions to exercises

Solution 2.1

```
type
    payment = (cash, cheque, credit, creditcard);
var
    transaction: payment;
```

The program extract becomes ...

```
case transaction of
    cash      :begin
                   {process cash transaction}
               end;
    cheque    :begin
                   {process cheque transaction}
               end;
    credit    :begin
                   {process credit transaction}
               end;
    creditcard:begin
                   {process creditcard transaction}
               end
end; {of case selection}
```

Solution 2.2

```
4.1    set action to continue
4.2    if score < 1
4.3    then
4.4        if score = 0
4.5        then
4.6            set action to analyse
4.7        else
4.8            set action to stop
4.9        ifend
4.10   else
4.11       if score > maxscore
4.12       then
4.13           set action to error
4.14       else
4.15           do nothing
4.16       ifend
4.17   ifend
```

Solution 3.1

(i)   valid. Loop is executed 3 times.
(ii)   invalid. *so* comes after *do* in scale order.
(iii)   invalid. *re* comes after *do* in scale order.
(iv)   invalid. *i* is of type *integer* whilst '1' and '9' are *character constants*.
(v)   valid. Loop is executed 26 times.
(vi)   valid. Loop is executed once.
(vii)   valid. The implicit definition of the type of variable *sex* places *male* before *female*. Loop is executed twice.

Solution 3.2

```
{update day} ... if day = sat
                 then
                     day:= sun
                 else
                     day:= succ(day);
{write out day} ... case day of
                     sun : writeln('Sunday');
                     mon: writeln('Monday');
                     tues : writeln('Tuesday');
                     wed : writeln('Wednesday');
                     thur : writeln('Thursday');
                     fri   : writeln('Friday');
                     sat  : writeln('Saturday')
                 end;
```

Solution 4.1

(i)
```
monthtotals = array[month] of 0..60;
```
(60 has been chosen as a reasonable maximum. You may have chosen another value.)

(ii) The index is apr, not 4.

(iii)
```
total:= 0;
for currentmonth:= may to sep do
    begin
        total:= total + monthtotals[currentmonth]
    end;
```

Here *total* is an *integer* variable and *currentmonth* is of **type** *month*. The **begin...end** pair is optional.

Solution 4.2

The solution is contained in Figure 4.9 in the text.

Solution 5.1

(i)
```
var
    page:array[1..120, 1..66] of char;
```

(ii) Along with the type definition

```
sex = (male, female);
```

the following are all plausible.

```
var
    table:array[sex, 1..6] of integer;
```
or
```
var
    table:array[sex, 'a'..'f'] of integer;
```
or
```
type
    bands = (a, b, c, d, e, f);
var
    table:array[sex, bands] of integer;
```

Solution 5.2

(i)
```
wanted:= 0;
for i:= 1 to 6 do
   wanted:= wanted + results[1980,i]
```
scans the 1980 row

(ii)
```
total:= 0;
for i:= 1976 to 1986 do
   total:= total + results[i,1];
average:= total/11
```
scans the pass grade 1 column

Solution 5.3

```
        set found to false
        loop for all rows
           loop for all columns
              if current value of items
                           = searchstring
              then
                 set found to true
                 set row to current row
                 set col to current column
              else
                 do nothing
              ifend
           loopend
        loopend
if found = true
then
   write out col and row
else
   write out that not present
ifend
```

Note that this design is relatively simple; for example, if the *searchstring* is in *items[1, 1]* the use of a **for** loop means that the whole array is searched needlessly.

Solution 5.4

(i) We have to add up all the array entries except those corresponding to 0, 1 and 2 hours. For this we require three nested loops (which can be given in any order):

```
set total to 0
loop for ages from 13 to 19
   loop for both sexes
      loop for hours from 3 to 8
         set total to total + survey[age, sex,
                                        hours]
      loopend
   loopend
loopend
set percent1 to total/10
```

Note that the final value of *total* gives the total number out of 1000, which is converted to a percentage by dividing by 10.

(ii) This time the value of *sex* is fixed at male so we have just two nested loops:

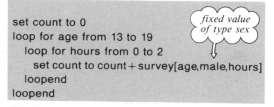
```
set count to 0
loop for age from 13 to 19
   loop for hours from 0 to 2
      set count to count + survey[age,male,hours]
   loopend
loopend
```
fixed value of type sex

(iii) This time the *age* is fixed at 15 and *sex* at female, so our count is achieved by a simple loop, over the full range of values for hours

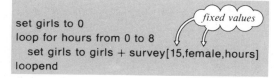
```
set girls to 0
loop for hours from 0 to 8
   set girls to girls + survey[15,female,hours]
loopend
```
fixed values

Solution 6.1

Identifier	Type
classize	integer constant
marks	array[1..classize, subjectlist] of 0..100
pupil	array[1..classize] of string
overall	array[1..classize] of 0..100
rank	array[1..classize] of 1..classize
subject	variable of type subjectlist
classno	variable of subrange type 1..classize

Solution 6.2

```
2.2.1    set sum to 0
2.2.2    set number to 0
2.2.3    loop for all subjects
2.2.4       update sum by adding current mark
2.2.5       if mark <> 0
2.2.6       then
2.2.7          increment number
2.2.8       else
2.2.9          do nothing
2.2.10      ifend
2.2.11   loopend
2.2.12   if number > 0
2.2.13   then
2.2.14      set mean to sum/number
2.2.15   else
2.2.16      set mean to 0
2.2.17   ifend
2.3.1    set average to rounded mean
```

Here we have used the following additional
variables

Identifier	Description	Type
sum	aggregate of the pupil's marks	integer variable
number	number of subjects taken	integer variable
mean	mean mark before rounding	real variable
average	rounded mean	integer variable

Solution 6.3 _____

```
top:= 0;
for classno:= 1 to classize do
  begin
    if overall[classno] > top
    then
        top:= overall[classno]
  end;
position:= 1;
repeat
  count:= 0;
  for classno:= 1 to classize do
    begin
      if overall[classno] = top
      then
        begin
          rank[classno]:= position;
          count:= count + 1
        end
    end;
  top:= top − 1;
  position:= position + count
until position > classize
```